Barely Out of Training

Cara Biceffi

Dedication

This book is dedicated to anyone who ever wanted to give up but persevered through

Acknowledgment

To all the people who I met throughout the years which inspired the story you are about to read.

Contents

Preface

This book has evolved through my personal journey spanning months and years across different countries and continents. Along the way, I've had the privilege of meeting a handful of extraordinary individuals who have faced their fair share of challenges in love, ultimately emerging from the other side stronger.

Together, they have collectively shaped the essence of the characters Paige, Mia, Damien, and Four – one day, they effortlessly inspired me, only to present challenges the next.

It is my hope that you will enjoy their company as much as I did and that their stories will resonate with you during your own twists and turns of love's journey in your life.

Chapter One

Damien – The Trap

I was fortunate to sleep the entire flight. Anyone who has been through a few hours in the air knows that flights are brutal if you don't like them, but I haven't seen my pops in person for about three years now, so it has to be done.

My Dad left when I was about nine years old, married Anna, and moved to her country to start a new life. Anna was married once before and has two kids from that marriage. Rob and Mia.

I only keep in touch with Rob, but we don't chat that often. He plays hockey professionally, and I follow football, so that's that.

I hope we'll hang out when I get over there, but Rob already warned me that we might just end up working throughout the summer and hauling logs down the forest to the landing spot known as a Trap.

Anna inherited that place with many acres of land after her first husband passed away.

Finally, we landed, and I saw Rob standing by the arrivals area before I got through the passport check. He is much taller than I expected, and he is ripped.

When coming closer, I see a scar on his temple that wasn't there before, but he looked dangerous even without it.

The only one speaking in the car on the way is Dad, whose mouth is unstoppable for kilometers and kilometers, giving me a headache.

"You have the same bedroom to the right, or you can sleep at the lake house. Take your pick," he sends my way once we enter their house. I am barely paying attention as I just spotted a friend of Anna's that she is speaking to in the kitchen, and wow. That chick is really hot.

Wait, did she just call her Mia? Oh, that's my stepsister. She was fourteen the last time I saw her and definitely looks different now. Just like the girl who used to be the screen saver on my phone. Damn, she is hot.

I waved at her, but she ignored that, and I noticed Rob signaling me from behind her back to let it go.

After a while, Anna turned around and said something while looking at me. Based on her gestures, I understood she wanted me to go to bed to rest.

Why did I agree that they would only speak in their language so I could try to learn it again? Total BS.

"No need, I… okay!" was the sentence I put together out of the few words I remembered from my last visit, but I must have hit the right vocabulary as Rob pushed himself from the table to say,

"Exactly, no need! Let's go to the Trap."

"You'll meet the guys," he added while taking cookies from the plate in the middle of the table, then nodding first at me and then towards the door.

I follow him outside, where he starts urging me on with more gestures. As I said, he is a heavy hitter, so I move where he points. No questions asked.

Then he mumbles, "A decent ride, right?" And with that, he smacks the hood of the car we are getting into.

"Mia is pretty," I put together once we set off, and he responds with a load of words in their language that sounds like a machine gun. "Well, that's sensational too. Trust me, I can see her with someone like that, and it won't go well for any of them."

I am not catching a single word of it, but he suddenly looks angry, so I quickly nod to show him I agree.

We had already parked at that point and were getting out of the car, and yes, the Trap is still dope.

It is a large timber harvest surrounded by acres of forest running along a massive lake at the bottom of a mountain.

I stood there with my mouth open for a while before realizing Rob was already walking the shore up ahead, so I ran after him. And there, we met with the first guy.

"Hey, finally showed up again?" He leaves those words in the air when throwing one of the logs onto the splitter, and then he looks my way.

I actually remember this guy. He is annoyingly good-looking, and his eyes are hard to forget. They are extremely blue, almost unnatural. He goes by his nickname Four. He is Rob's best friend and has that presence about him that even when he stands alone, you think there is an army behind him.

He is an ambulance driver, and even though he has been helping the family for years with the land work and stuff, he is not on our payroll.

Apparently, he is highly paid at his EMT job even though he drives like a maniac, or at least that's what Rob once mentioned about him in a text. *I guess it's a bit like a Russian roulette when you call in with your emergency. Four will drive you to the ER or straight to the other side. Either one.*

I smiled at him, but Rob also turned his way and said, "Hey, they said no speaking English to him."

"Oh yeah, right," Four agrees, and I see his arm muscles flexing when he throws another log.

Shit. There is no way that I can do anything like that. I only hope that they realize it as well.

We moved again then, and I still followed Rob like a lost puppy. We are getting closer to their lake house. It is newly built and three-story overlooking the lake. *Dope.*

"Where the hell are you all at? We need stuff for the kitchen!" says Adele, who showed up at the door. A girl with blond hair pushed back into a ponytail. She has a few more pounds on her than I would typically go for, but it suits her. I remember her from when we were young. We used to fish together and never caught anything.

"Hey, I am Damien," I blurted out stupidly, wanting to quickly remind her who I was.

"Hi," she basically whispered.

"And me, well, you can call me whatever you want," comes back but from another girl. A redhead who sticks her head out of the window to check me out. I learned later that her name is Camilla. She moves her ample cleavage to the side and asks Four, who caught up with us and now stands behind me, "Does he understand me?"

I turned that way and was faced with Four's electric blues when he asked, "You remember some of the words, right?"

I have no idea what he wants, so I smile.

He grabs one of the drinks standing on the table. Then he raises his eyebrows, sarcastically stating, "Well, you'll be useful to us then."

I smile at him again, for that might have been the correct answer before. By that, my eyes meet with a guy sitting on the bench in the corner. His name is David, and he is Adele's brother.

Most of his body is covered by tattoos, and I believe he used to be a boxer before he went to jail for driving under the influence more than often. He is ripped.

What the heck? Is everyone around here working out twenty-four-seven? Never mind, I prefer to stick around the ladies anyway.

They are both working here whenever they can, mainly helping with the meals for the workers.

As I said, every hand is needed around this place, with a lot of hard work waiting.

Perhaps one of the reasons why I don't visit that often.

Chapter Two

Damien – Settling In

As predicted, the following days are hell. I almost wish that I would suddenly come down with a serious sickness of some kind, so they'd have to pull me out, but so far, I look healthy. *Shit.*

The afternoon heat gets to around thirty degrees daily, but it sure feels like fifty from where I am standing, so I try to keep in the shady forest as much as possible.

My hands are ripped to shit because I didn't like the gloves I was given yesterday, and I was pulling without them. I was counting every minute and couldn't wait for my break. When it finally came along, I walked deeper into the forest, found an excellent hiding spot underneath a bush, grabbed my snack, and finally chilled.

"What the hell you think you are doing?" yelled Four, who I see now sprinting my way from who knows where. When he got to me, he added, "This is not a freaking vacation, you feel me? You must keep close to me. You and your stupid chicken strips are sitting here and waiting for wolves. Are you crazy?"

So, eating alone in the woods here must be out of the question. Perhaps next time, he could yell at me in English.

When we got back to the Trap, the girls were already packing up to get all dressed up for a disco party we were apparently going to that evening.

I keep rubbing my eyes; the sweat around them burns as hell, and I am just not down for anything tonight, but it's not like they will ask me about that, so I guess I am going.

Four got a call and had to return to work, so I am now pulling the endless shift with David and Rob alone. I am literally at the end of my rope.

I had just unchained the last two logs from the tractor when I noticed Rob nodding to the lake. Then he shouts, "Let's go."

You are all mental around here, but swimming will get some of this sweat off me, so why not?

His massive arms are already working their way through the water in the lake when I'm gently stepping in.

Fuck, this is cold.

I thought about my next move, whether I would do it or not, and stood there for a while. A girl walking the shore strolled up to me, and I was definitely checking her out. She had black hair, big earrings, and a sunburn on her back, and she smelled great, might I add.

I stared at her for a while, so she started speaking slowly in their language. The words sounded like, "Hi, you are the stepbrother, right?" but I wasn't sure if that was really what she said.

When there was no answer from my side, she waved towards the water and added, "Are you going for a swim?"

Oh yeah, girl. Now I get it, and I am down.

And we get things going in the water a little bit, and I like kissing her lips, but then she says, "You have to go," while looking back at the lake house.

I also noticed David calling my name from somewhere over in that direction. Still, I was not moving for whatever he wanted. She started pushing into me, saying, "Shoo, shoo."

"All right, all right," I gave up then and started moving out of the water. I found David sitting on the terrace by the house, vaping while waiting for me.

There was no point in yelling at Rob deep in the lake, so we left without him. On the way, David pulls my T-shirt occasionally, pointing me where to go and making me feel like a dumbass.

When we get to the disco, I can't see shit over the smoke, but David finds the girls somehow.

Mia is definitely the prettiest girl in the hood, but she is also turning out to be a bit weird.

I know I don't speak their language, but she has not said a single word to me yet, and I know that she graduated in English, so I get it, Mia. This is personal.

Chapter Three

Mia – About the Colors

Rob went swimming yesterday, and apparently, the lake is getting warmer. I can't wait to go for a swim as well. I long for the minutes in the water and the feeling of complete freedom it gives me. No words, looks, judgment, or other people.

They are all too colorful and much to handle in general. My world was much easier before I learned about the colors and energies that everything around me has. It all changed on the night of the crash.

It was just me and my Dad in the car that night. We were visiting our grandparents up in the mountains, and they all thought that I had food poisoning, so Dad was driving to the nearest hospital to get me checked out. As some sad, stupid movie would have it, it was pouring rain, dark, and the road was covered in puddles. It only took one wrong turn too close to the edge, and we were falling.

My family thinks that I do not remember anything, but I do. More than remember. I can see it all, and it feels as if it happened just yesterday.

Seeing my Dad's eyes in front of me, his hand reaching out to my car seat, trying to protect me in the last moments of his life. I am screaming, trying to grab hold of his hand, and then everything goes black.

The hospital stay after that is blurry, but the sadness remains. The feeling is still wrapped around my lungs like a deep, slow burn. It wakes me up in the morning, my mind knowing that I had the same vision in my sleep last night as every other night before. Still, as much as the constant replay hurts, I do not want it to go away as it keeps him alive, and it keeps him with me.

This was when it all started. When I returned home from the hospital, I said to my Mom that she was yellow to me. My brother had a red color around him, and he still has it to this day.

As time went by, I kept saying weird things about the colors and feelings of other people's energy, so my Mom had us visit many doctors and many brain scans. Still, nothing out of the ordinary was found.

No explanation for the way I see and feel this world.

All these feelings come in at the same time. Noises, voices, smells, auras, energies, and together, create a vast sensory overload that is very hard to manage; sometimes, it is too much to even think about.

A person can be brown and cold to me, as well as brown and warm.

I made my specific color and felt chart based on a personal experience with a particular type of person. I would never speak to someone with a blue aura and cold energy, as well as I know that I am in love with the view of a red aura combined with the feel of hot energy, which I have only one example of outside of my brother.

The one and only Four. An adrenaline junkie and my brother's best friend. *How typical.*

Of course, he would be the one with the right color and feel for me, but I don't predict anything will ever happen between us as he is just not interested in me. That fact has been torturing me for the last two years, having him in front of my eyes almost daily.

He is simply gorgeous.

A broad-shouldered guy with sun warmth, tawny muscles, and a dark-toned face shaped by brown hair that just falls carelessly into the view of his intense blue eyes. Eyes that only make one angry when covered as not giving the chance of staring at them together with the beauty of this man. He is ripped all the way down to the "V" shape, where his pants hang low on his hips, and his body only adds to the combination of the perfect face with high cheekbones. Then, there is his energy. Damn. That constant pumping high, combined with the red aura around him. You can search this Earth through and through, but there is no other like him.

He has been my dream and a nightmare all in one, knowing that I am, by that fact, simply unmatchable, but one day at the hospital where I work as a nurse, I was given the gift of another hope.

That night, a girl was brought in with a leg wound and a high fever, and I kept an eye on her the whole night. I was more than happy to. She was fascinating to me. Her aura was red, and her energy hot.

Her meds kicked in in the morning, she felt better, and we started talking. Her aura's color didn't go away as I feared it might, and she just stayed fantastic. We remained friends for the rest of her hospital stay, and I knew right then that I was even falling for her.

So, there will never be another Four, but there might be a red and hot soul somewhere out there that can tolerate and even love my weird existence.

Chapter Four

Paige – The Club

I should reach the club in about twenty minutes, but only if the traffic stays reasonable.

Carly texted me as she was already there and super excited. The guy she has been in love with for at least the past six months is coming in tonight. He is a hockey player. I think his name is Rob, and he is fit. I give her that, but hockey players aren't really my thing.

Rob tips well and spends a lot of money on the girls, but then he always has at least two in his bed for the night. Even though Carly is usually one of them, I am sure it doesn't mean much to him. Only she thinks it does, but that guy is unstoppable on and off the ice and literally breathes adrenaline; go figure.

On the other hand, Carly is one of the girls dancing in the bar, but she also goes with guys for money. She seems to make a lot, so her outfits are always on point, and I sometimes borrow clothes from her, just like I did today. So, I know the drip on me is dope, and I feel good.

But I am not part of their game. I am not chasing the money and most definitely not sleeping with anyone. I have been positioned as a bartender for the last eight months by the private agency, the

RF, which raised and trained me at the nearby military base, and I am just waiting. Waiting for my actual assignment.

Sometimes, I fear it will never come and my training will all go to waste. All the time on the mats in the gym, endless hours in the field, and the water will account for nothing. I hope not.

There are two private military agencies in the area competing against each other. The Pollwest agency drafts cadets who already served in the army and have obtained their training there. Then, there is our agency, the RF. They scout prospects from anywhere and are willing to train them. Just like they trained me. They taught me everything I know and provided me with room and board, but now they own me. I would never put enough money together to pay them back for all they have done and become free.

Once again, I watched the floor at the bar all night, ensuring I was spotting everything and everyone. Still, none of the elders showed up to assign me, so I had nothing. The word within the base is that I am the last unassigned cadet of my training level. *Shit.*

Carly's hockey player, Rob, showed up around midnight, but she had already gone with another dude. She will be pissed about that tomorrow and will probably cry as well.

Rob sat at the bar for about an hour, watching hockey highlights on the TV behind me and drinking with the other hockey dudes.

He left me a pretty generous tip while looking me up a few times, and I had to admit again that he's hot. I even caught myself being glad he would not be my mark, for he is not significant enough.

Once my assignment comes, I am sure I will go after someone important, like the president of a big firm or a lawyer messing with our agency.

I remember clearly the first day I saw the RF military base. At that point, I still couldn't believe that I had won the draft and actually got in, and I was shaking like a leaf.

The girl I was competing against was physically much stronger. What got me in at the end were only my academic test results and the speed of my hands.

While being locked in the basement of the house of my foster care, I have been throwing a bouncy ball that I found on the street for days and days. I could catch that little thing flying at me from any speed and angle.

In the evenings, when little to no light was coming in through the window, pointing at people's feet on the street, I kept throwing and catching into complete darkness.

Eventually, I was kicked out of that house and transferred again, but the next placement didn't work out well for me either. After that, I vowed I'd never go back into the system and ended up living on the street when I was fourteen. There, I met Ted.

Ted was also newly homeless. He was a sad and quiet man who had just lost his job at the University due to his drug problem. That also caused him to lose his wife, his house, and his kids.

We ended up in each other's care. Ted was my protector, and I was his when he was high and unable to function. Yes, I was stealing for us so we could survive, and when Ted was sober, he repaid me by giving me an education.

We spent hours in the public library together, as Ted used to teach the girl at the front counter, so she let us come in without having an access pass.

I lost contact with Ted when I joined the RF. I searched the streets through and through after I passed the initial stage of my training and was able to get out for a few days, but he just vanished.

I didn't find our tent at the park, and none of the people on the street nor his drug dealer could say where Ted had gone.

After that, the base became my home, and I have become possessed by being the best at any level I could.

I would take extra sessions in offered lessons to secure my spot amongst the boys coming in. After all, I am just a girl.

I don't have the same muscle and body type, but I am fast and still throwing my bouncy ball at any free second I get.

Chapter Five

Damien – A Gift In Yellow

"You reek of alcohol," declares Anna towards Rob and Four sleeping on the floor in the living room, which makes Four move his ass, and then he also takes the blame for it when saying, "I had a couple of shots yesterday."

She raises her eyebrows, adding seriously, "I hope you weren't driving the ambulance."

"Nah, I parked the medic at the Trap," he gets out with a scratchy sound in the back of his throat. Then he looks at me while moving his head to the side as if measuring me up before turning back to Rob with a question, "Are you sure the dude is all good up there? He smiles like an idiot, and he smiles all the time."

Rob doesn't answer. He is watching my pops moving things into his car outside, and then he mumbles, "Well, you would have to ask the boomer over there."

With that, he starts putting stuff that we will need down at the lake into my hands, and today I know that I am wearing the damn gloves, no matter how sweaty and filthy they are.

When we got to the lake house, Four went through the drawer in the kitchen and handed me a SIM card. He was already turning away from me when he pointed out, "That way, we'll have a chance to get a hold of you if you decide to have lunch in the woods again."

I slide the SIM card into my phone, and everyone comes over to type their numbers into my contacts. David, Rob, Four, Camilla, Adele, and I also get Mia's number. *Cool.*

I was hoping to hang around the girls for a while, but Four is already calling me from outside to join him, as our target is to do two trailer loads full of export logs this week. Those logs are cut to a container length for shipping and are the hardest for me to work with. I like the Chip-N-Saw or Pulpwood type of logs as they are much shorter, and I usually don't screw anything up when moving them around.

At least this time, Four lets me drive that heavy skidder through the harvest, and I feel like a king as that machine is a beast.

When we reached the end of the logs area, Four pointed his index into the distance just beyond the trees, and I spotted a bear walking out of the forest.

"He's not scared," I pointed out in a surprised tone, and Four smiled when he answered, "Nope, but he's hungry. I bet he is ready to share if you bring some chicken strips."

"Ha, ha, ha, very funny," I say while driving the skidder quickly away from that area.

When I returned back home, it was already dark out.

I found a yellow T-shirt laying on my bed, and apparently, Mia got it for me.

I do not know why she thinks I like yellow, but whatever.

It is a friendly gesture so I can wear this shit to make her happy, and maybe she will talk to me before the summer is over.

Or maybe not. *What a weirdo.*

Chapter Six

Mia – A Night Visit

I am only checking on patients for a dermatology ward today; the shift is dragging on like crazy, and even the bus ride home takes forever.

After dinner, I started watching a movie, but I don't think it was very good because I fell asleep in the first few minutes.

Suddenly, a sharp light hits my eyes, and I hear Rob's voice in my room. "Sis, get up!"

He can say whatever he wants. I am not moving my hands from covering my eyelids until he turns the damn light off, but then he goes again. "Come on, Mia, Four needs stitches."

And that does it. I am officially awake.

Four is now also in my room, with blood seeping through the left side of his shorts, and it sure looks like there is a severe wound underneath.

Hold on now. Just because I fixed a few hockey cuts and wounds doesn't mean I can handle something like this. That's way out of my league.

"Come on," I hear Rob's nervous voice again as he tries to push me into action. I know him well. He will not stop until I go along with this, but I only look angry at him and shake my head.

Meanwhile, he walks over to the window. I hear two or three police sirens somewhere in the distance. He lifts the corner of the blinds and turns back to say, "They seem angry. Is that for you?"

Four smiles and admits, "Probably." His energy is pumping as the aftermath of a police chase that he was obviously the reason for, and I can't get enough of him.

At that point, Rob looked at me again, but I was still in the same place, still shaking my head, so he came closer and urged, "Mia, I am not kidding, help him!"

With that, he pulled the blanket off of me, and I was on my feet immediately and crossing my arms over my chest. His stupid brain should have remembered that I sleep topless.

"Oh, sorry," he said, but I was already moving to the bathroom to put something on. I growled back at him on the way, "Get him some clean shorts."

I look around the bathroom but see only my hospital scrubs. There is no other option; I must put them on. Four smiles when I return to the room and says, "I guess you saw me coming."

I grab my old sleeping bag and some towels and throw them on the floor. I don't really want to, but I also put the gloves on. Rob returns with some clothes; I take them from him and place scissors in his hand instead.

He comments, "Great," but surrenders and kneels to Four, who is already half lying on the floor. Rob cuts his shorts through the side and stops just under the waistband, revealing the whole length of the wound.

It starts on the top of Four's muscly thigh and runs all the way down to his knee. Some pieces of asphalt were jammed under his skin, with blood coming to the surface around them already, creating a severe bleed, but the worst stands in the middle of it all. I see a pretty deep cut, good for six or seven stitches, with blood steadily pumping out of it.

Rob makes a retching sound and looks to the side to say, "Yep. I am gonna be sick."

"Keep it together! What's wrong with you?" comes from Four, so Rob forces himself to look at the wound again, only to shake his head and mumble, "Dude, that is disgusting."

With the next retching sound, Four rips the scissors out of Rob's hand and commands, "Get out!"

"You bet," Rob covers his mouth and runs out of the room.

Now, it's on me to kneel next to Four and tell him the bad news. At this point, I am sure there is no way I can do anything about this; it's just too much. Before I'd say it, though, I felt his hand on mine.

I look at him, and on top of seeing his handsome face, he adds the voice that I cannot resist, saying, "Mia, if I go to look for a doctor now, the cops will have me in a second. I am gonna do time."

His touch is burning me up inside, and I would love to help, but I just can't. I shake my head again.

"Please, Mia, can you just close the cut? That's all I need," he begs, and my decision to have nothing to do with this is already falling apart. I get up then and go back to the bathroom to look through my stuff.

When I return, I hand him two of the strong painkillers that I was given by the doctor last month before he cut my wisdom teeth out. Four smiles again, and I almost melt to the floor under the blue of his eyes when he says, "Thank you."

The night is one of the longest.

Rob got picked up by his hockey buddies and went clubbing, but I am keeping an eye on Four until the morning. Thankfully, he didn't get a fever throughout the night.

The dish full of the asphalt pieces removed from his skin now sits on the floor beside him. I wait another hour or so, then lean over to check on him again but see that he is now awake. He doesn't say anything; he only moves closer and, then out of nowhere leans in to kiss me.

I always knew if that was ever to happen, I would be lost forever, and I was right.

At that moment, all of my love for him, worrying about him, and wanting him got together like an uncontrollable wave of emotions, and it's not only about the red aura and hot energy anymore.

Now, thousands of electric sparks have taken over my body, and nothing other than being with Four makes sense.

"Well," he says when he pulls away, adding a smile. He runs the top of his fingers down my jawline before he adds, "Hi."

I only bite my lip a bit as I can hardly do or say anything now. *There is definitely no point in pretending that I am not into him.*

"We lock the door if you want and get things going. I'm down," he offers; I run my eyes over the state of his, under normal circumstances, strong body that is lying there in front of me now between the pile of bloody towels, only to say afterward. "You are crazy. Shut up."

I add a tired smile, but if we were in his apartment instead of my room and if I hadn't just placed eight stitches on his left side, oh, help me, God.

"And so, she speaks," he almost whispers when placing his head on the pillow again and falling asleep almost at the exact moment.

Chapter Seven

Damien – The Disco

I would have slept longer, but guys are making noise in the next room, and it is only getting louder. How much I want them to shut up, plus, I don't understand what they are doing in Mia's room anyway.

I pulled a blanket over my head, but that didn't help much as Rob's voice came through the wall from right behind me. "Dude, that was just nasty. I don't know where Mia gets the stomach for that."

Four mumbles back, "I had to jump a ditch and crash it. Otherwise, the cops would have had me."

Rob laughs when adding, "You are nuts, bro."

"Mia knocked me out with opium or something super strong anyway, and I had some crazy dreams, man. One, when I thought I actually kissed her."

"You would need more stitches than that if you did," Rob responds before adding, "but that was pretty stupid giving you the meds. She could have killed you. I bet you were already high when you got here."

I understood some of it. What the heck is happening in this house? I know Mia works at the hospital. Is she giving them drugs?

When I get downstairs, Rob throws an apple at me from the kitchen, testing my hand and eye coordination like he tends to do sometimes, but I am getting better at it.

"Four isn't coming. He pulled a muscle last night," he says, but the only thing out of it that I understood was some undertone of anger in his voice, so I nodded and smiled again, as that seems to be a good answer for everything around here.

Then we get back to the Trap, and as the girls now told me in English, Four won't be helping today. Out of all days. *Shit.*

We barely spoke to each other for the rest of the day, finishing up as soon as possible and dragging ourselves to the disco again. The night was getting long.

Camilla seems interested in talking to me and has been yelling words over the very loud music for a while now.

She asks if I know where Rob is. It's still easy to pretend I don't understand any of their words, plus, it's not like I would tell her about the blondie riding Rob outside in the car for the last half an hour anyway. It seems she wouldn't take it well. Maybe jealousy or something.

Anyway, I am glad their language is coming back to me. Slowly, but still. It is a final payoff for times when I missed my pops and was trying to learn to speak it so I would feel closer to him and maybe even move over here one day. *Pathetic.*

Suddenly, we hear a scream from the bar, and the DJ stops the music.

One of the girls from the bachelorette party broke a glass and stepped on a piece of it. I don't faint in the side of blood, but damn, there is a lot of it.

They patched her up a bit, and then we all waited for the EMT to arrive. It didn't take them long, so it was easy to guess who was on a shift and driving tonight. Four even came up to the disco hall with the paramedic.

He was limping, so he must have actually pulled a muscle for real, just like Rob said he did. It is weird to see him in the uniform, and I think the girl next to me watching him is just about to faint. *Also, pathetic.*

"Do you know him?" asks a girl behind me. When I turn around, I see the face of the cutie I kissed at the lake the other night and haven't seen since. Her name is Sabrina.

She let me kiss her a few more times that night, and it felt pretty good.

Chapter Eight

Paige – Fresh From The Fight

The sun is not out yet, which is great because I plan on running to the first mark of the mountain before it comes up. I am sprinting between the trees and already feel the muscle burn in my thighs, which is what I was going for. Great.

I need to reach the viewpoint within the next ten minutes if I want to watch the sunrise from there, and that should still give me enough time to get back down for the morning call at the base.

I like to train with the newbies. Those cadets who have just been drafted. They have that extra adrenaline within them when trying to prove themselves to the leaders, and I feed off their energy.

I made it to the viewpoint ahead of time, but still, the sunrise is shit today. The clouds are rolling in before the thunderstorm, so screw this. I am heading over to the base.

I put my hood on before going through the scan, as everybody does at the front gate. We go through facial recognition anyway, so there is no chance of anyone unauthorized getting inside.

Today, they got us new spec-ops masks for the drills, and I already don't favor the orange-colored shield, but whatever. I will just have to deal with it.

Before we got on the field, I learned that I was assigned to a new training level. That means I no longer recognize the body shapes of people around me.

I have been training with the same team for the last three years. Somehow, we all knew each other even though I'd never seen their faces as we were all masked up. None were here. I must have been the only one who moved up.

This is all new to me, and the tempo gets faster as one of the leaders decides to join in for the second half. It's almost impossible to keep up with this guy.

I am sliding through the obstacle course behind him, chasing him, and he is making every move a true challenge for me.

At the last stage of the field training, we jumped a fence, sprinted through a tunnel, and stopped when we reached the place set up for our mini battle. It is a multi-story building that looks like an adjoined apartment complex.

My lungs feel like they're ripped in half, and I am gasping for air, but I don't want the leader to see it. He is wearing a mask and colored shield glasses, but somehow, I feel his eyes on me. I am new to his team, so that would make sense, but I find it very intimidating regardless.

We wait for the others to join us, and then he is called back to the other leaders.

I am being lined up with three other cadets. One is a weak

link, but the other is a solid trainee with improved skills and helps me carry the other over safely.

The leader slapped my shoulder after the drill when I walked to the building to return my fatigue, so I guess that means I didn't do badly today. Still, I hope he is coming back tomorrow because he brings a new level of excitement to my training, and I want to continue to prove myself.

I feel overwhelmed by him and honored to be here again. There is something about his presence. He is dominating and powerful.

My leader in the previous team was all right. He was patient and calm, maybe in his thirties, but my new leader is not like that at all.

He is definitely younger and might even be my age. He is in the best form, but it is not only that he is ripped that is intimidating. He is very skilled, of course, but there is also that weird presence about him. As I said, dominating.

I still had about an hour before wanting to leave, so I changed into my gym clothes and mask and then hit the gym.

I am here by myself, and I love the peace of it, but within the next twenty minutes, the room starts filling up with people.

I stay for another half an hour or so, but that weird feeling of someone watching me through the two-way mirror of the second floor gets even stronger now and kills the vibe for me.

It makes me move to the other room, which is the last one, before exiting the building, and thankfully, no one is in it. Just an empty room full of lockers.

I stop somewhere in the middle, get my bouncy ball out of my locker, and start throwing. The room is not that big, and it makes the ball bounce around at a perfect speed; when it ricochets off the walls, it flies back at me from any possible angle, which is the feel I need. I love it.

I get completely lost in my game and forget about time or anybody else standing and watching from behind the two-way mirror above me.

It was like my therapy, but I still managed to get to the shift at the bar on time.

It is now 10:45 at night, and I have been getting drinks for these four guys sitting at the bar for at least three hours now. As time goes on, the alcohol is changing them into the type of men I hate to work around.

The men must have come in right after watching a sports game in the city, and their anger is coming into the bar with them as clearly, their team didn't do well tonight.

It is always the same with guys like this.

It starts with a few drinks, which gets them rowdy, and they slap the ass of a girl or two on the floor, and it ends with them being thrown out.

"Hey, green eyes, bring me another drink," one of them already shouts in my direction, and this one seems to be the loudest today. He looks at me like he owns me, but only I know I could break his little neck without much hassle. I stay calm, smile, and place the drink in front of him.

There ya go. Snap, you would not even see it coming.

"And what about me, ya little slut," calls out one of his friends, and with that, all of them start laughing.

Keep it steady, Paige. Just go get the drink.

In the corner of my eye, I see our bodyguard moving closer, which makes me slow my hands down in the middle. I don't want to waste my time. They are all about to be thrown out anyway.

I played with the straw in my hand to stall the time, but then an empty piece of glass flew through the air and hit the wall just a few centimeters from my shoulder. The broken pieces fly everywhere, and then I feel a little burn on my hand. Everyone knows the feeling once the skin gets cut. *Yep, that's the one.*

I duck down and turn around to take a look at the same time.

The bodyguard is in front of the bar now and tries to take

control, but he is alone, and there are five of them. Things are starting to get heated, so I am just thinking about calling the cops when I hear the words coming from behind me. "Stop ignoring me, you bitch!"

The voice makes me turn that way, and my eyes meet with the guy who wanted that last drink and is now rushing my way. He is yelling nasty words, walking even faster, and getting himself pumped.

We are not supposed to show any skills, that I know, but will I let this idiot mess up my face? I don't fucking think so.

I don't see any other option than to defend myself in the only way I know. He is literally sprinting around the bar now, and he is coming in fast. I smile.

In my head, everything goes quiet. There is only him and me. He is reaching out towards my throat, but in the way he stands there, I don't see any skills, so I am guessing he will get his ass kicked. At the exact second of me stepping back into my weight and getting ready, Rob jumps over the bar and knocks the guy down. He must have just gotten here because I did not see him before now, and I also see his teammates running our way.

With the hockey players involved in the fight, more people are joining in, and I am about to be done with this. I can't have any more stuff broken. Let's call the cops.

But just when I am about to dial, Rob's huge hand lands on mine, and he says calmly, "No worries, we got this."

I never fully realized how tall he was until I saw him standing beside me. I am staring at him now, like a schoolgirl; I don't know for how long until someone threw a bottle at us, and on top of all that, he now covers me with his body.

Damn, Carly. I completely get it now. Your obsession with him, all of it. Rob is sexy as hell. It's a shame that I couldn't offer him anything other than a drink, so that's that.

Chapter Nine

Damien – The Bartender

Depending on Rob's hockey schedule, either he or Four takes us to the Trap in the mornings, and today is Rob's turn. We pick up Four on the way. He is still limping heavily, and overall, he looks like he was hit by a train.

I am sitting in the back seat of the car and looking into the car mirror so I can fix my hair, then I notice when Rob spots that. I know he was about to comment on it, but his phone rang before he could. He sees the name on the display, makes an annoyed face, but leaves it connected to the car.

The guy on the line starts fast and angrily, "A bar fight? Really? What were you thinking? You are on the contract. If you get injured, we are all a shit out of luck."

"Okay, yes, I know. Relax, I handled it," Rob says, scratching his head.

"Next time you are going to call me, the Mayor will skin me alive if anything happens to you," the guy on the line demands before adding with a softer tone, "But other than that, thanks for saving the girl."

Rob smacks his lips before he asks, "What girl?"

"The bartender. She said you saved her; she would have been hurt otherwise."

"Oh, Paige, yeah, no worries," says Rob while hanging up on him, and it's only a second before Four goes with a fishy tone, "A bartender?"

"Oh man, do you know Paige? The bartender at Steve's? Everyone is trying to tap that. She is super-hot. Even I was about to go there and make her sweat, but I guess I am getting lazy. My girls are booked, and they just know what I want."

Four smiles and slaps Rob's shoulder when stating, "Dude, you are so screwed. You'll never settle. It takes two to put you down, but no, I don't know Paige. I don't go to the bar at Steve's. We have booze in the basement when we play cards there."

With that, we reached the Trap, and I got out of the car fast so I could walk over to the house before them two and park myself into a chair on the terrace.

David eventually comes over with his vape and sits his ass down in the chair beside me. I don't mind this dude, but I hope he will not try any more of their words on me this morning because I am tired of smiling.

"Are we going now?" comes from Adele, who is now standing at the door of the lake house and nodding towards the lake.

Oh yes, we said we would go for a swim, and yes, what if we would get something going. I am down.

I started after her, but in the middle of the move, David grabbed me and brutally sent me back to the chair, with which I began to fall over.

He growled, "I'd hate to see you closer than a meter from her. Are we clear?"

I grab the table before me at the last moment and gain my balance again. "We do nothing together!" I spit out quickly in their language, as he was obviously getting a little aggro.

"Get out!" he adds disgustedly but letting me go.

They told me about their rule of not going after anybody's sister, but are you kidding me? What was that about?

There is nobody else around here, and the redhead Camilla would squeeze the living shit out of me, so what else am I to do?

Chapter Ten

Mia – A Bookie

I love running the shore in the morning when you hardly meet another soul outside. I had been running for about twenty minutes, and I was almost at the train station when I heard the sound of a motorbike coming from behind me.

It must be Four. Sigh. The last thing I need is the torture of looking at him, but hey, it's not him.

This is the guy with a tattoo on the back of his neck who whizzed past us on the bike the other day while we were driving to the shopping mall.

He stopped the bike now, and he was so close that his shin touched mine when he took his foot off the foot peg.

"Fancy seeing you here," he chirps, and by that, he changes his aura from friendly yellow to sweet orange. Still, there is a strange tone in his words that makes me start to move away. He reacts to that with, "Wait, I told your friend I wanted to talk to you."

His energy is even more calming, so he's got my attention, but I still look at him suspiciously. He smiles and adds, "I did, really. I spoke to the red one with the big bumpers."

Using his hands, he's creating an image of big breasts in front of his chest.

He obviously spoke to Camilla.

With that, I started walking, so he pushed the bike to keep up with me and said, "Oh yeah, you don't talk much. I heard."

That statement saddens me, and I am about to be done with him, but he adds, "Hey, don't get me wrong, that is exactly what we are looking for. You know, someone who can keep a cash count and their mouth shut."

I stopped walking, encouraging him to add, "You'd be a perfect fit for us. I think. Well, you can come with me tonight, and you'll see."

His name is Mateo, and he picks me up in the evening at the bottom of our hill as agreed.

On the way, he asked me to grab his bag from the back seat and hand it to him. He goes through it and pulls out a black wig and stupid-looking sunglasses, like those you would win as the lowest price at some country fair. He gives them to me before the bag flies back onto the seat behind. Then he says, "You need to put them on."

What now? Is he serious? Maybe getting into a car with a stranger was not the best idea. Am I being kidnapped?

He then points to the back of the car again and says, "If you get thirsty, there is water in the trunk. Don't take no drinks and no drugs from anybody. That is how we lost the last girl."

Now, it is confirmed. I am to be locked in the trunk of a car and probably sold to some drug dealers. It is so weird, as it doesn't feel like he means me harm. His aura is yellow, and his energy is friendly and calm, but maybe I am reading him wrong, and whenever he takes me, they are going to kill me.

"I told you not to bring your cell phone earlier, right?" he asks, and even though that is just another red flag, I nod.

"Good. The race would be canceled if you did, and we would pay a lot of money to cover the losses."

Wait. Did he just say, "the race"?

Mateo is a spotter.

His job is to pick out a car, which the racer must steal on the day and bring it to the start line, but Mateo will not tell me this. I learned it from the other spotters when we arrived at coordinate A.

We hang around there for about thirty minutes before finally receiving more information. There, today's race starts from the old armory, about 17 km from us.

The racers will be using route 112 all the way to coordinate B. Still, the exact info of the finish line is, at this point, only given to the racers and the more important people. *We ain't it. Obviously.*

Mateo and I are among the first arriving at the armory. I see a line of people in front of the gate who are only missing guns in their hands to pass for a SWAT team.

They all seem to wear the same black uniforms, masks, and

baseball caps. We are being spotted by two of them. It is a man and a woman. They point to a spot on the left, and Mateo pulls over. He stopped the engine and got out, so I did as well.

The guy runs a frisk on Mateo, and the woman searches our car. Then she approaches me and pats her hands all over my body. She is very thorough. I swear the sides of her hands touched my no-no square when she was going up my inner thighs. She then gestures for me to remove the sunglasses and the wig. I do that happily.

"What's your name?" she asks. Mateo reacts quickly and says, "Trinity."

I then put the stupid drip on me again, and we joined the other people who passed the check and are now standing by the garage doors at the back. After that, it is just a long wait again.

Between the conversations, I hear that the racers in the stolen cars will get here just before 8:00 pm. That is only if they do not have cops on their tails, as they cannot bring them to us. Even then, everything must happen in the blink of an eye, just in case the cops snoop around.

Finally, the lot is filled with people, and we are opening the bets up. That is the task Mateo brought me here for.

So, from now on, I am being called a bookie or Trinity, but at least I am not getting murdered. Phew.

I wish more money was won by the girls who come to me

shyly with their small bills rather than the guys who throw rolls of money at me, barely saying a word and acting as if I should know who they are and who they are betting on.

Mateo comes to me as well at one point.

"Do you have it all?" he shouts over the noise from the crowds while glancing at his watch. "He'll be here any minute."

Who? I wanted to ask, but then I saw two cars driving in the distance along the long fence enclosing the armory parking lot, and as they reached us, their energy stopped my words.

Both cars look like they were already racing on the way here. There are grass stems and mud dropping out of the heat of the bumpers, and loud music is playing in both cars. The drivers shout at each other through the opened windows, and the rush of adrenaline that suddenly fills the air is just indescribable. Still, what shocks me the most is that all of it feels nice to me, which is the opposite of what I usually get from such an amount of overload.

Now, I feel great. At least until I recognize the car's driver on the right. He has a mask on his head, but I know his energy, build, and his electric eyes.

The guy is Four. Shit. Of course, he is! How could he ever not be part of this? Now what?

My heart reacts and starts pumping the blood brutally all

the way to my neck. I try to take a step back and hide in the crowd. Ouch, I got hit in the eye with a money roll.

"I have it on Four, "a guy yells from the left, but I don't get his name; as the circle around me is closing at that point, the crowd is pushing me from side to side, and I am running out of oxygen.

I am saved by Mateo's hand grabbing mine, who just shoved his way over to me while pushing about two bodies away from me, he holds out five hundred in the air and says, "Put it for me on Four."

Meanwhile, another two cars pulled in, but there weren't many bets on them. Then I hear the gunshot, indicating the start of the race. One of the guys comes over to me and throws some keys and a phone on my laptop.

"Take my car and bring it to the finish," he shouts, hardly caring if I know how to drive. The phone screen is lit up with coordinates. It must be the location of the finish line. I nod unnecessarily as he is, at that point, far gone, and I start walking over to the last three cars parked there.

With a push of the remote on the keychain, an Audi R8 convertible flashes at me, and I truly hope that at least this car wasn't stolen.

I didn't see Four that night again, as he did not reach the finish line.

In one of the sharp corners, he flipped his car upside down, but I heard in the crowd that he was laughing at it all, so I guess he must have been high again.

Thankfully, nothing serious happened to him.

Mateo then finds me behind the line and helps me with all the payouts. On the way home, we didn't talk at all. He was arguing with someone on the phone in a language I didn't understand.

Once we reached the bottom of our hill, he gave me my money cut and grumbled that he will send me a message for the next time.

Really? Do they want me there again?

My hands are shaking.

Wow. So much money!

Chapter Eleven

Damien – The Fight

It was the first time I slept at the lake house, and although it didn't seem that bad on the floor at first, now I feel like shit.

Rob can sense it, I guess, as he slaps my shoulder right when I stand up, and he tells Four, "He looks like he's dying. Take him with you, would ya?"

Four nods, grabs my T-shirt, and pulls me towards the door.

"Come, we need to go get some stuff," he says, and I follow.

He takes Rob's car, and right when we get on the main road, his phone rings through the car speakers. Four answers and the guy on the other end asks if he is free to talk.

Four says, "I have this guy in the car, but he only speaks English, and he is dumb as shit, so don't worry about it."

The other guy laughs and asks, "So, what the hell happened to you yesterday?"

"The car broke down on me," Four responds with a smile.

"That's cap. I heard you went straight to the donuts and couldn't keep it on the road!"

"Well, I always do a little blow before, you know that," says Four while taking a turn so fast that the side of my face hits the window next to me. Then he asks the guys, "Did Three finish?"

"No, he had the cops on him, so he had to drop it."

After that, there is a moment of silence before the guy asks, "Did you see the new bookie?"

"Yeah, in a blurry. I was kryptonite."

"Dude, there was so much money on you, plus, you should see this hottie, Trinity. I think Chris brought her. She was driving his car."

Four smiles again and says, "Trinity, eh? Give me a week. She'll be sitting on my face."

"Well, first, you get your ludes straight, all right?"

"Yeah, forget about it," says Four while hanging up on the dude, and I continue to pretend to be observing the horses on the files as we go by.

Four looks at me like I am an idiot or something and says very slowly in their lingo, "Grass. Horses. Pretty." I just nod and smile back like I truly am the idiot he thinks I am.

The day went by with a blink of an eye after that, and we even got to the disco pretty early, but I was just ready to go home. *There is no way I can survive the whole night in here! I am barely standing.*

Suddenly, I felt someone right behind me touching my back and shoulders. I whipped around to see Sabrina standing there smiling and I was instantly riled up, so I grabbed her hand. Rob, Four, David, and the girls walked past us at that moment.

Rob snaps his fingers, then points over towards the stairs. Although it makes me feel like a dog jumping on a command, I follow them anyway and drag Sabrina along with me.

Once again, she doesn't expect much from my lingo, which saves me from the small talk, and my hands run all over her. The night suddenly makes more sense, and I don't feel that tired anymore. Then when I am trying to suck my lips on her again, she turns my head towards the direction of the door.

There, I see my brother pushing a guy out into the hallway with full force, and Four is already limping his injured leg over there as well. At the same time, David taps on my shoulder, but I react quickly in English and say, "No, I don't fight," while adding a heavy tone to the next word. "Never."

"Well, tonight you are," David says excitedly while literally ripping off his T-shirt and pushing me out of the room. We then ran down the stairs and forced the entrance door to open for both of us.

The cool air washes over my face only seconds before the hit comes. My ears are ringing now, my vision is all hazy, and I feel disoriented as hell.

Then another hit gets me straight between the eyes, and I am now bending forward and covering my nose. I feel a push from behind, and I run into the guy who must be the one who just punched me. We are both falling to the ground. I can see blood dripping down from my nose, and I start throwing punches.

After some time, the guy kicks me off him and runs away to the bushes. I turn around and see Four, Rob, and David already gathering back together. Outside of Rob's T-shirt being a bit messed up, they all look like they just left a spa resort.

Why am I the only one bleeding here?

"Well, no wrist shot for me for a while," says Rob, who's smiling happily and trying to fix his right hand by twisting motions before he spots me and points at the blood stains on my hoodie, asking, "Didn't cover your face, did you?"

"There was no way to see that one coming," David stands up for me, and Rob comes closer to assess the damage on my face. He states, "We'll get the guy back for that, don't worry."

"That's okay," I say quickly because there is no chance in hell that I am fighting any time soon again.

"No, little buddy. It is NOT okay," he returns with that tone that prevents any follow-up, so I must let it go.

I then headed for a restroom and found a shady one. I tried to get the stains off the hoodie, but I only made it worse.

When I finally got out, an order came from Rob, and the group started rolling back to the Trap. I decided not to go back with them. I went back up to the disco hall and found Sabrina instead.

After we dance for a few more minutes, I suggest we leave now, so we start walking the path back to the Trap. Sabrina saw me touching my nose at some point, so I said, "I don't even know why Rob started it."

She replied, "I know that Alicia, a girl I went to high school with, was sitting at the bar; some guys were hitting on her. I guess they slipped something into her drink when she wasn't looking. Rob must have seen it. He came over, told Alicia not to drink it, and then dragged the guy out of the room. That's when you got involved."

She pronounced the end about me somehow proudly, so my ego flew through the roof. I stopped her from walking, put my hands around her waist, and leaned in for a kiss. She let me dominate it, my tongue searching hers, and I felt the pressure pushing onto my zipper already. When we stopped kissing, she started giggling and running down the path of the wooden dock leading to the lake. *Fuck. I hope she doesn't want to go swimming. That shit is cold.*

Thankfully, she stopped at the end. I followed her down the dock, turned her back around towards me, and started to kiss her again. My pulse kicked up a couple beats again, and I was not waiting for anything. I slowly put my hands under her bra. I started playing with her nipples a bit while she grabbed the top of my jeans, pulling my zipper down. Before I knew it, my pants and boxers were down around my ankles.

A smile came to my lips with the thought of the shittiest place that we have chosen for this, but whatever, I am not backing away now. She let out a hard breath when my fingers traveled down between her thighs. I felt them sinking into the warmth, and I started pumping in and out, as I have seen in those movies but other than that, I didn't know what the fuck I was doing. Though, she seemed to be liking it, so I kept going.

Soon, she pushes me to lay down on the dirty and slightly moving dock, but whatever I lay down. She then sits right on top of me and takes me in.

I start counting to thirty, hoping for the best, but her breathing is also coming on faster. Hopefully, I can last at least a few minutes. I am touching her soft legs while she is moving up and down. Then, out of the blue, she erupts, and it doesn't take more than a few shakes of her body, and I am goner as well.

Rob greeted me happily when I made it to the Trap.

"There ya go, little buddy. Something for the slow one," he says and hands me a bottle that smells like something fruity, I guess it's some type of girl's drink, but whatever. I take it anyway.

However, I wasn't finished with even half of it when I spotted Four. He was clearly already wasted. He usually doesn't go down that easy, so I ask Rob. "What's up with him?"

He turns around and says, "English is not allowed, brother."

Really? Why is he being annoying now?

"What is. About. Him?" I tried slowly in their tongue then, but not sure if it came out right.

With that, Rob looks at Four, sitting on the other side of the room by the window, chugging down the rest of the whiskey bottle that has been glued to him tonight. Rob whispers my way, "Four was called to a bike crash today, and the dude died on him in the ambulance. You know, this shit will go down no matter how fast he drives, but he blames himself if they die on his watch."

I step towards Four to say something to comfort him, but Rob's hand flies in out of nowhere and lands on my chest with an impact that almost takes my breath away.

Then he says, "There is no point in trying, brother. He needs to deal with this on his own."

Chapter Twelve

Mia – A Stray

Mateo called me a few times. I couldn't answer, so I texted him to meet me when I got off the bus.

He picked me up, and we drove to a gas station. There he threw some phones into my lap, saying, "Those are all clean and untraceable. Pick one, and you can bring it to the race, but don't keep anything personal on it."

I nod and say, "Alright."

"Four was asking about you. He wanted to know who you are and if you belong to Chris, but I said you belong to nobody. You are a stray."

A stray? Really? But wait, actually, why not?

I turn to him and say, "Yeah, let's keep it that way."

He moves his mouth to almost a frown before he says, "Okay, but listen, it's best not to mess around with him. Four is a beast. Being high all the time, he has no control. That's how he wins every freaking race because he doesn't give a fuck if it is his last ride or not. It's better to stay clear of him. Ya hear me?"

I nodded to that and already started to feel excited about the next race. The only thing I loved more than the money Mateo had given me was the feeling of complete freedom while being Trinity.

The girl that nobody knows.

The girl that can do anything.

The girl that relieves me from Mia's life, at least for a moment.

Across the parking lot at the gas station, I notice my half-brother Damien meeting with two guys, Knox and Drew. Both of these guys have a terrible reputation around the hood.

"What are you looking at over there?" Mateo asks suddenly; I shake my head and then try to turn my attention to him again. I don't want to stare in the direction of where Damien is standing, but I can't help it.

What are they up to? I didn't realize they knew each other.

Mateo is then ready to leave, but I start asking unnecessary questions about the payouts to prolong our stay there while watching Damien in my peripheral vision.

So far, he seems to be only smoking weed with those guys, but he could have chosen a better company for that.

Am I going to rat him out to Rob?

You bet I am.

Chapter Thirteen

Paige – The Fight

I am so grateful that the leaders moved our training inside the base today, as it has been raining the whole night.

I changed into my training clothes and entered the gym. A few guys are sitting in the corner around the treadmill area and nod at me as I walk by, so I guess I am making friends around here.

I have seen them in the bar hanging around Carly a few times, but I would never take my mask off here. So, they have no idea who I am. However, they should also be wearing their masks. It's a rule of the program; it's a rule of the base. They can get kicked out for this.

At the exact moment of my thought, a man enters the room and angrily commands, "Full battle rattle." The words are coming through his mask, and the built-in voice changer in it gives me chills.

I haven't heard this man's natural voice and probably never will, but somehow, I know it is my new leader before I even look that way.

Then I turned around, and yes, it was him.

The first view and judgment of the leader's demeanor might consider him arrogant, but then why shouldn't he be? I have seen him fighting a handful of times, but he is by far the most dangerous person I've ever met.

The guys are startled and quickly put their masks on while he walks by. I am so happy he is back. He missed a few sessions. I assume he had been away or suffered some injury.

He appears to be stepping more lightly on his left leg. Then, it must be an injury, perhaps from the fights.

At that point, he already entered the next room, and the connecting door of the two gyms loudly slammed behind him.

One of the other leaders then directs us to start the exercises as marked on a screen at the back of the wall. Together with the numbers of our training tank tops, we picked up at the beginning of our camp. I took number thirty-six.

Once we complete enough exercises to gain twenty points, we can move to the next gym and work with our leader.

I have been missing two points for a while now, and most of the guys are ahead of me and already going to the next gym. *Damn it. I must get my shit together.*

Still, even though it made me angry with myself for not reaching the next level as fast as the other guys did, now it's evident that as quickly as they went in, at the same speed, they were coming out.

"It is not possible to fight with him today. I had to tap out," comes from one of the two cadets walking back towards our gym.

The guy next to him, who entered right after, adds, "I did as well. The leader was livid. Did we piss him off that much, or what is his deal today?"

"No, it's not us," answers the first one. "I heard the other leaders talking, and they said something went wrong in his personal life. Someone died or something."

The second guy rips his mask off in frustration and adds, "Well, somebody will also die here today if he keeps going like this."

"Wait," he says then and stops his gaze on me. "Girl, you are not going in, are you? You are fast, I give you that, but this is a different league. He is not in the right mind today; you will get injured."

I take another two steps, so he tries again and says, "You are crazy. I honestly wouldn't go in there if I were you."

Crazy? You have no idea.

With that, I am opening the door to the next room.

I walk in and see my leader on the other side. I am heading his way.

He is facing the wall while drinking from his water bottle and, without even looking at me, already raising his fist to his shoulder level and thrusting it upward to the full extent of his arm and back to the shoulder level several times to signal to increase my speed.

Wow. We truly are in a bad mood today, aren't we? Still, I do as he signaled and hurry up.

I got over to him, and then he turned around and recognized me. It is easy to tell, as it cannot be anybody else. There is only one other girl at this training level, and she has more muscles on her than half of the boys in the other gym.

"Finally," comes through the leader's mask, and even in the disguised voice, I feel a smirk behind his tone when he adds, "Couldn't get your points any faster?"

I guess he is trying to piss me off. Well done.

"Did you miss me?" I reacted without thinking it through first. *Shit.*

"Watch yourself there, cadet," he responded right away. With that, I noticed how his posture differed from the other days I'd seen him fighting. Today, he is already in the pre-fight mode.

He then relaxed his broad shoulders, and I started watching him even more closely. The way he controls his breathing, as well as how he manipulates the distance between us to stay in proper range.

I haven't fought him yet, so I don't know if he means to be a striker or a grappler in our fight, but no matter what, I think his stand here today is to fool me.

He puts his water bottle down on the floor and takes a few steps into the room. He wastes no time and points for me to take the floor as well.

I followed his motion, and we started walking fast in a circle. He lifted his fists and increased his speed but did not give me anything else to work off of.

I noticed only that he stepped pretty low to the ground, almost like dragging his feet.

Dangerous, but guess what? I've been stupid before, and I will be again. I am going for it.

I take two or three fast steps toward his left side; I strike and hit. I wish I could see his face or at least his eyes to see a reaction to it. Still, he wouldn't fight without his mask or take his colored glasses off, which other leaders tend to do, so I think something about him might give out his identity. A tattoo? A scar? His nose? His eyes?

At this time, he is already on the move, which is the worst. He is gaining speed and any angle he might want, so this whole thing stopped looking good for me right before this moment.

Then he attacked, and I struggled to defend myself.

Big time.

My hands are moving fast, but I am getting hit a lot and quickly feeling exhausted while he dodges most of my hits.

I managed to get through only about five so far, but at least they were well-aimed.

I hit him again. *Ouch. It's like punching a rock.*

He is getting more and more frustrated and impatient with me by the second; I can feel it.

Still, that is where I want him.

At the point where he will slip up and make a mistake, leaving himself open. He then suddenly gets a grab on me so strong that I can't twist out of it no matter what I do, and I think I might pass out.

"Am I talking to myself around here?" he asks. I understand he referred to his training about two weeks ago regarding this scenario. He showed me personally about three ways to get out of it.

Come on. Think!

I then twisted my hips and dug my chin down to create that extra breathing room while hitting him under his ribs and getting out of his grasp. *Hell, yeah.*

I felt great and powerful; plus, on my way out of his biceps, I elbowed the front of his neck quickly.

The hit must have browsed over his Adam's apple as he is gasping for air now and losing his balance.

I pushed his body away from mine and thought about the next move that I could use to knock him out, but with that push, he reached the right angle and space to kick me in the chest. *A forceful blow. Fuck.*

I will not be able to breathe deeply for a few days, that's for sure.

I am trying to balance myself, but already feeling dizzy. He is still gasping for air and dropping down to his knees.

I hit the floor and tap out. I might have seen him about to do so as well, or was I already dreaming while passing out?

When I opened my eyes again, I was lying on what looked like a surgical table, and the medic's face showed up above mine in a distance too close for my taste. He asks, "Are you all good now?"

I nod and ask in return, "Is the leader ok?"

His answer is, "Of course," but with that, I suddenly feel that I probably shouldn't have asked such a thing, so I add quickly, "Can you not tell him that I asked?"

He runs his eyes over the two-way mirror of the second floor as if he could see through it or get a signal from up there before responding with, "He already heard you."

Of course, he did. I should have remembered the eyes and ears of this place.

62

Chapter Fourteen
Damien – The Speech

Four, Rob, David, and I were working pretty deep in the woods today, pulling logs to the road up the hill. At some point, Rob turned to me and said, "I heard you picked up some new friends."

And I know what he means.

Sabrina introduced me to her two buddies. Knox and Drew. It happened at the gas station where she wanted to meet me.

Knox is a tall dude who seems pretty ripped. The other guy, Drew, asked me the same thing Sabrina did when she saw Four pulling into the gas station with his ambulance to get gas.

"Is he your friend?"

"I work with him," I answered, and Drew added, "Well, Four is interesting. I've seen him arrested for stuff at least three times before. My friend is a cop and checked it out for me and guess what. There is not a single record on Four for some reason. How come? Can you find out?"

"We are not that close," I said, but Knox turned to Drew tiredly when lighting up a joint and added, "Don't bother, Drew. It is not him. I told you. Look at this guy. He is an ambulance driver; of course, there is no record. Cops, medics, and firefighters all cover for each other; plus, do you know what would happen if Four was held overnight and missed a race? People would break the jail down. But he is not who you think he is. Do you really believe this idiot could tap me out? I can promise you, Four wouldn't even know what the basic M-9 pistol is and for sure couldn't take it apart or use it. He is a loser."

"I don't know, dude. There is something about Four," Drew judged again just before Knox tapped on my shoulder. "Alright, then. Damien here will keep an eye on him for us, right?"

I didn't like Knox's face or gestures even before he said, "You will do it because you wouldn't wanna be on my bad side, would you?"

I smiled at him in return because that was all I had.

So, to answer Rob right now, truthfully, I wouldn't say Knox and Drew were my friends, but the way Rob and Four were looking at me right now was kind of cool, so I said, "Yeah."

"Don't let them pull you into any shit. They are a couple of idiots," comes from Rob, and I think he needs a chill pill. Knox and Drew aren't that bad. They seem fine to me.

I meet with Knox and Drew right after dinner in the forest behind the same gas station we met earlier today. Though, this time, it is obvious we are not buying anything.

We smoke some weed and drink some booze, and then Knox goes to the trunk of his car and pulls out three masks and two guns.

What the actual fuck? Is this the type of shit Rob had in mind when he talked about them earlier? I guess so.

"No way," I say, but Knox is already pushing me out of the bushes in front of him, saying, "Come on. You are only a lookout, so relax."

At that point, we are getting out of the forest area and into the light surrounding the gas station, so, exactly as Rob said, I am being pulled into this shit.

I was left outside armed with nothing while those two ran inside to rob the damn place.

The guy at the till is taking his time to give them the money, or that's how it feels from where I stand watching this whole thing down. There was no one around when they went in, but now I see the headlights of cars in the distance on the highway heading our way, and I am freaking the fuck out.

Finally, Knox and Drew came out of the station with a few handfuls of money, and we started running towards our car.

When we got back in and drove away, I yelled at them. They both seemed to ignore me until Knox turned to Drew and said, "Make him shut up, would ya?"

Drew hands me a portion of the money, and they both think that fixes everything. It doesn't but I am too tired to argue.

Chapter Fifteen

Mia – The First Time

I am getting into Mateo's car confidently today and with my sunglasses on.

"Wow", he says the second I get in, but I look at him, confused, so he adds, "They are all saying how hot you are, and now I see it too."

"They? Who?"

"Oh, girl. Everyone," he states before adding, "Though, there are some shady characters there, so watch out, all right? Just keep your eyes on the money."

I nod. And we then don't come back to that conversation, which saddens me a bit because there was someone I wanted to ask him about.

A girl who, last time, literally took my breath away. A small, energetic bookie with beautiful lips. She might be a mestizo, even though she wore a blond wig. Her aura was friendly orange, but her energy was simply indescribable.

Then we finally got to coordinate A, the Medieval Fortress in the woods. I saw the girl again right when we passed the security check. She is talking to the guy who let me drive his car last time. He waves at me, so I go over to them.

"Hey. I hear you are Trinity," he affirms, and I nod.

"I am Chris, and this is Izzy. She takes the right side of the track today, and you are on the left."

I reach for the laptop that he is giving me, and Izzy smiles at me before she says, "Nice to meet you. I'll see you around, Trinity."

I smile back and feel the heat on my face. *I want her. Dah! Of course, I do.*

Throughout the next hour or so, I learned that Izzy would take me to the finish line after we wrapped up here. This time, I was paying more attention to the people around me.

Most male spectators wear masks or bandanas covering their faces, as barely anyone wants to be recognized and connected to the auto theft racing. Still, a few guys seem to be of a higher rank within their gang, and they just don't give a shit about being identified, so their faces are barely covered.

I know at least three of them here tonight whom Adele's uncle, a cop, put in jail for unlicensed gun possession a few times already.

Finally, Chris gets some info, and we are told to open the bets. On my laptop screen, I see that Four grabbed his car successfully and he is in the game. The only one missing is alias Six, who didn't manage to snatch the chosen car, and the note said, "a pit bull," so I guess he got into dog trouble.

Then Chris leans closer to Mateo and says, "Four ditched the cops about five kilometers away. Alias Three is behind him and says that Four is coming in hot. ETA is two minutes."

The guy who was hanging out behind their backs is now moving away. He lifts the megaphone to his lips and announces loudly. "Two minutes on Four."

With the last word, the crowd goes wild, the music gets even louder, and the girls start pushing each other and moving closer to the track. I hold the laptop with all my might, making sure I won't drop it. I am then pushed back from where I was standing, which helps me hide in the crowd, but when Four shows up, his car is on Izzy's side anyway.

After the race started and Four was gone, I immediately walked over to Izzy. She was talking to Mateo, who was collecting the money from her. Before I got to them, they were both sniffing a line of white powder from the hood of his car. It must be coke.

That makes me not want to get in a car with her, but then she points to her BMW, and I follow her anyway. *There's no helping it; she is just mesmerizing.*

However, the conversation in the car didn't go as well as I hoped. I guess I am not as good at flirting as I thought I would be. *Shocker.*

By the time we reached the location of the finish line, I was sure I had blown it with her, but after the payouts, she came over. She pulled me to her and started kissing me.

I felt her lips moving on mine, but I also noticed the white powder she had all over her mouth and tongue being rubbed onto my lips and then into my gums.

I would definitely keep things going with her and do more than a kiss, but the fact that my mouth is super numb now makes it impossible to make a move. The only thing that overwhelms me is the urge to drink any liquid on site. *What a weird mess of feelings. I can't wait for the after-party.*

I want to keep talking about anything and everything. I want to keep smiling and maybe dancing, but I am also getting weirded out and even paranoid. I want to keep feeling confident, happy, secure, and pleasant, but it's hard because I need to do all of that at the same time. It freaks me out again. And yes, in the middle of this all, Four finds us kissing on the hood of her car.

Izzy moves her lips away from me to say, "Hey, Four, nice win again," but I don't give a damn about him right now. I still want to do anything and everything and keep moving. Still, she seemed interested in talking to him, so I left them to it and walked over to the trunk of her car like I was looking for something, but I was not.

"So, she likes girls then," comes from him, and Izzy replies, "Yes, sometimes."

That reveals what I told her secretly in the car, so I am not very happy about that, but I see Four biting the knuckles on his left hand before saying, "Oh God, that is so hot."

Izzy smiles at him again and says, "You are pathetic."

Four reacts right away. "Oh, I'll be pathetic. I am down for anything. She can do me over; I don't care. Where did she go?"

"Trinity," I hear Izzy calling my fake name, and the only thing I am stuck with is that I want to do whatever keeps me pumping. Four is still standing there, kind of in my way, and I realize again how freaking handsome he is.

The broad shoulders, tight muscles, and the most handsome face I have ever seen. And this might be my chance to get close to it all again, so I walk over to him and slide my tongue over his top lip. It's a part of that rush, and it feels incredible.

I hear him saying, "I think I am in love," while I am already walking away.

Izzy starts laughing, and then we get back to making out. Four then kind of joins in.

Chapter Sixteen

Damien - Fireworks

Dad brought us some fireworks and Four plans to show us all how it's done. He refused my help, which I think was a good choice, considering I know nothing about fireworks. I assisted him with his joint earlier, which should account for something.

Four comes back to Rob and me. He lands his ass next to us so they can continue their conversation with Rob about stuff that happened last night. Rob starts with, "That's insane, dude. Where did you find a girl like that anyway?"

Four shakes his head in disbelief and replies, "Insane doesn't even cover it, mate. It's like you start the night with a V-card and end it with a freak. It got so intense that the other girl bailed out, we ended up falling through a glass door, and I got cut up to shit, but it was a great night. We've made good on both sides, but when all was said and done, she got kind of salty, like she regretted it or something. Now she won't answer my calls, texts, or anything."

Rob smiles into the dark and judges, "She sounds like a bitch." Four grabs a bit of sand into his fist and then throws it into the lake, looking frustrated, saying, "Trinity. Damn. I am hooked."

With that, Rob places his hand on the back of Four's head and shakes it a bit. "It looks like you are losing your mind for this chick."

Four continues to shake his head even when Rob lets go of it and states, "Maybe it was just the coke rubbing her the wrong way, you know."

Rob takes another hit from the joint and replies to him through the smoke. "Oh great. Another fiend. By the way, is there a race tonight? Are you going in?"

Four nodded before he returned to his fireworks prep, and Rob took that moment to turn to me and say, "Whoever that freak is, at least he's keeping busy with her."

In response, I use the only word from their language that I master and ask, "What?"

"Whatever keeps him away from Mia, we are okay with."

I look at him again and repeat, "What?"

He breathes tiredly and continues in English, "Yo, little buddy. Adele and I are the only reason they don't have kids yet. We keep them far from each other, and you should help do the same."

I nod and ask simultaneously, "What can I do?"

"Just make sure we know where they are and that they are not together. If they ask about the other, we say they are simply not interested."

"Okay," I say, as he thinks it has worked so far, and then I ask randomly, "Why is he wearing all white?"

"Yeah, that's a good question. Let's see," he answers me before turning to Four and shouting, "Hey, dude, what's up with the white? Are you the bride tonight?"

"Fuck you!" comes back from Four, but at that point, he finally finished the prep and then helps us get through two bottles of vodka. The alcohol got us into jumping Rob's buddy's broken truck until it stopped running completely, so Rob used some chalk from the lake house and drew a few targets on it.

Four then fired from an old shotgun through all the different parts of it, surprisingly, without a miss. Rob spotted my shocked eyes when I saw it happen and took another swig from the bottle in his hand before commenting, "Epic, right? Four sure knows how to put a bullet in."

I would have had some questions about that, but Four had already started the fireworks from the bed of the old truck. I decide to lie down in the sand, stare at the pretty lights, and grab a joint.

A kick to my foot wakes me up, and I see Four standing on my left. "Hey, little buddy, I've got to go. Rob has gone to see about some girl, but I can drop you off at yours if you want."

Firstly, I am sure he's as drunk and high as I am, so, "No, thanks," and as I slowly sit up, I now notice Knox and Drew standing by the end of the dock in the distance, obviously waiting for me.

"No, I am fine," I say, and then I watch him in his strange white outfit jumping into his car and disappearing into the night.

"What's up?" Knox greets me when I walk up to them. Then he starts walking away, so I follow behind.

We hop into his car and start heading down the road. After a few kilometers, Knox asks Drew, "Did you get the location yet?"

Drew mumbles something while pulling out a map. He circles a spot on it and places it on the dash before Knox. At that point, I had to ask because this was ridiculous. "You guys don't have GPS?"

Knox looks at me like he wants to knock me out and shouts, "You brought your phone?"

With that, he shoves Drew in his shoulder with a force that looks like it'll leave a bruise and yells, "You didn't fucking tell him not to bring his phone?"

Drew then raises his voice at me. "Where is your phone?"

"I forgot it at the Trap," I say in a low voice.

Drew answers with, "Phew. A close one. Do not ever bring it with you."

Okay, whatever.

The map then leads us through kilometers of the deepest

forest I've ever seen. I was almost sure we were lost, but we actually reached the place soon after.

It looks like some old ruin of a castle guarded by a line of people dressed all in black. We are ordered to pull over and park.

Knox does as he's told, and we all get out of the car. One of the guys from the line is wearing a bulletproof vest, which is weird as I see no guns. He is now walking in our direction.

He pulls me aside and runs a frisk on me.

When he's done, Knox throws me a piece of cloth.

I look at it confused, but at the same time, I see that it is the same mask that both of them are putting on their heads, so I do the same.

Knox comments, "I am freaking sick of wearing this shit on my head all the time. I had it on me the whole morning."

Why and where would he have to wear a mask? Was he robbing another gas station in the morning?

I follow them through the stone walls in front of us. Way before we reach the opened courtyard of the old castle, which is now damaged to the point that it looks only like the ruins, I already like what I am seeing. A big smile comes across my face.

I see girls, booze, and drugs; the air seems to be filled by all of it, and I am getting off on it even before I see my girl. Sabrina.

She has a red wig on and sunglasses, but their surface is so light in color that you can see an image of her eyes through them, and it's so sexy.

We then get some booze from the guys selling it out of their van parked by one of the walls. When we walk away from them, I notice that Knox seems pissed now, even more than usual. He explains those guys stole their gig tonight because the booze is what Knox and Drew normally supply to these things. Before I have the chance to ask what type of event this is, the courtyard gets filled by revving engines of three cars flooring it in.

Knox grabs me by the bicep as the aggressive crowd suddenly pushes me towards the cars. He says, "There is your friend Four," but he doesn't even have to say that.

I see clearly Four getting out of the first car. The white drip is shining on him, and even though he is also wearing a mask, there is no way he can hide his build even if he wants to.

"He's got some balls," comes from Knox, and I look up, so he adds, "The car is nicked. Only Four would wear white when stealing a piece worth almost half a million. He is one crazy motherfucker. I give him that."

I am finally putting two and two together, but I still ask, "A race with cars that have been stolen?"

"Dah. Pay attention," comes from Drew before he takes another hit out of his vape. I don't get to say anything back through the noise of the revving engines.

We don't follow the race as the others do when the race starts. Knox isn't in the mood.

We just stay behind and smoke some weed before heading back home.

Chapter Seventeen
Mia - Busted

Damn, my whole body hurts.

Last night was out of control. Four is super fit and literally unstoppable, but he was lucky that I was too busy with Izzy's lips and his hands working on me at the same time. Otherwise, I would not let him enter me. *I still can't believe I ended up with Four's size, taking my virginity. Crazy.*

Thank heavens, I wasn't sober at all for that because when he entered me, it was so painful that I was about to stop the whole damn thing, but then suddenly, the pain went away, and it started to feel really good. He found my spot and got me going until I came with a scream from the overwhelming surge of pleasure combined with his energy.

It was simply amazing, but now I am barely moving. Plus, I am a bit pissed with Izzy for using me the way she did, as Mateo called me this morning to say that she actually has a girlfriend, which I had no idea about, who will beat the crap out of both of us if anything was to happen between us, so it won't anymore. The main question still remains, and that is Four. What am I to do with him?

He has been calling and texting all morning. Even after all

we have done together, he truly has no idea who Trinity is. He was obviously coked out of his mind last night, and it's clear that he has a drug problem.

I had Mateo swear to me that he wouldn't say shit, as I am planning on telling Mr. Four everything myself. After the next race, he will know who Trinity is.

I plan on breaking his little filthy dream as now he is on the hunt.

On the hunt for this mysterious Trinity. When he learns that she doesn't exist and that he spent the night only with little Mia, as he's been calling me for years, the chase and interest will be over.

Mateo texted me the info for tonight's race, but I can't go. Mom made me promise that we would spend time together tonight, and I couldn't talk myself out of it.

Now, I am on the bus taking me home. It finally spits me back at the bottom of our hill, and I am dragging myself to our house.

I see Dad leaning over our lawnmower when I get to the driveway. He looks up when I get over to him. "That old beast. It's choked up again," he points towards the grass cutter before redirecting his eyes towards our garage. I see Four coming out of it with a toolbox.

Crap. What is he doing here?

He nods at me, and I nod back while basically running towards the house away from him. Mom, whom I meet at the door, slows my getaway a bit when she says, "There is some chicken on the stove for you."

I keep walking and almost reach the kitchen when I hear her again, saying, "The door is open, and please use the green towel."

I turn around and see that she is speaking to Four now, who is coming in with his hands dirty from oil. His T-shirt is sweaty on his back, he is damn sexy, and I can't take my eyes off of him. *Shit. I need him out of my head.*

Mom pushes the vertical blinds out of her way and then turns towards me, her gaze landing on the right side of my body. Her eyes widened in horror before she asked, "Oh Gosh, Mia, what happened to you? Look at those cuts!"

I look at my leg, and my mouth reacts with, "Oh yeah, I fell through some glass yesterday; I am okay, though," before my brain catches up to what I just said. I look back at them both and find the blue of Four's eyes piercing through me like a knife. *Busted, he knows now.*

Oh, no, I can feel the spike in his energy. He is super pissed.

"You did what?" Mom asks, but I am already passing them

both and speed-walking upstairs. Somewhere in the background goes the repeat of her speech about me not being careful enough.

I ran myself a bath and stayed in it for a long time to ensure Four would be gone before I got out. Meanwhile, a message landed on my phone, and yes, it was from him, of course.

It says, "I think we need to talk, Mia."

"No, we don't," I respond quickly, holding my nose and leaning back into the water until my body is fully submerged.

Chapter Eighteen

Page – The Scraps

Many days have passed since our fight with my leader, but my chest is still in pain from his kick, and I am not allowed to enter the battle again until the pain has gone completely.

Meanwhile, I have been watching him on the field with a different level of recruits, and his speed and the way he fights take my breath away every time.

He noticed me once when leaving the fights. He walked past me but only asked, "Are you bored?"

I watch him until the door slams behind him, and disappointment washes over me.

Oh my God, what was I thinking? That we are friends now or what? I am an idiot.

I then go back to the gym and start to beat the shit out of the punching bag to get my frustration out. In doing so, I attracted the interest of one of the guys working out on the other side of the gym. He walks over to me and says, "Hi, I am Knox."

Then, he points the finger at his friend standing in the distance, saying, "That's Drew."

I look around in panic.

Why would he tell me his name? They are not allowed to share that information, only with the people with whom they share the room at the barracks.

"Good form," he adds while checking me out.

"Thanks," I managed to say, but a second later, a whistle blew in the corner of the room. Then, I see my leader walking towards us.

He stops next to Knox, but his disguised voice is directed only to me when he says, "If you are asking for help, I am right here. If you are asking for attention, do it elsewhere. Your time is up."

Ok, that is noted, but he needs to take a chill pill.

However, he at least saved me from dodging any other Knox's lines in the future. Knox ran away with his tail between his legs before the leader even said the first word to me.

I hit the shower, changed, and on the way out, I picked up an envelope from the office with my next little task.

It is an equation problem.

I used to be good at those, but today is just not one of my days, and I know why.

It is because of this weird inner shake that is taking over me lately.

Thankfully, the leader walked away from me right after what he said.

Otherwise, I would have probably started to defend myself, pointing out that Knox started speaking to me and not vice versa. Though I know how bad I am at those conversations. It would probably only make things worse.

Now it's obvious what I must do. I need to get my muscles moving again. I need a girl's time.

I already know where I am going. I will join the city's East side, where the scraps are happening. Those are the street fights that always end in many ways.

Last time, it got into a dust-up with the cops, but I don't need any of that today. I want a fast fight and keep it under the radar.

I used the few minutes I had to get myself pumped up. I then joined the rink and won a couple of rounds. My knuckles were really busted up by the time I was back in the car and on my way to my place.

I will pay for the broken knuckles tomorrow if the medic lets me fight again, but for now, I feel great. I got my anger out, at least for the time being.

I drove home, got baked, and finally solved the freaking equation problem. *That's right. I still got it.*

Chapter Nineteen

Mia– Grandma's

I must pack my stuff for a week at Grandma's, but it is the last place I want to go right now. Thankfully, Rob is also coming for at least two days between his games.

I like my grandmother, but I am pretty sure she doesn't feel the same.

She greets us with a smile and immediately grabs Rob with her wrinkled hand and chirps. "Oh, Robbie, we watch you with the girls, and we never miss a game, I promise you! And why didn't you bring Damien along with you?"

"He is working at the lake today," Dad returns somehow seriously.

"Well, I hope he comes to see me at some point. I wouldn't even know what he looks like these days," she follows up and then glances my way. I was about to reach for a hug, but then I put my hands back to my sides when I felt the drop in her energy.

No, she does not like me, for I am the reason why her son isn't here anymore.

She says coldly, "If you want to go outside, you can go to the river. It's not a lake, but you can swim there too."

I nod and walk back out the door.

I walk around the village briefly and check out the river afterward.

When I return, I find a message on my phone. It's from Adele. *"Can you please tell the "hockey prodigy" to call me back? Things are going sideways here; I need to talk to him. ASAP!"*

I looked around for him, but he was not in the house. I was about to ask Grandma if she knew where he was, but she rushed into her room before I had a chance to say a word, and she basically shut the door in my face. *Lovely.*

I then sit in Rob's room with my back leaning against the wall and wait for him while listening to Granma's phone conversation with our Mom for about ten minutes.

Rob climbed through the open window just as the last few words were said. Grandma stated, "I thought I could do it, but I can't. I don't want her here. You must come and take her back home."

Rob grabs me and pulls me onto his chest.

"I'm sorry, Mia. Forget about her," he says, pulling a joint out of his pocket. He offers, "Do you wanna get stoned? It might help?"

Yes, that seems like a great idea.

The next day goes the same way with her, and by the afternoon, it's clear that Grandma is spending the whole day at her friend's house to avoid seeing me at all.

Thankfully, Mom shows up around 5:00 pm, and I hear Granma talking to her and Rob downstairs for a while, but she makes sure to be gone before I come down.

I then get into our car and don't say a word.

Chapter Twenty

Damien – What About the Base

Rob sends me to help Four with the tree limbing, so I follow the chainsaw sound up to the highest level of the forest. I find Four above the caves on the rocky side of the mountain, where he's been slicing through the branches for the last two hours. He doesn't look like he has broken a sweat.

Drew may be right when saying this dude is doing more than just driving an ambulance. I also call that BS.

I started skidding the logs with the compact tractor again, hoping I wouldn't get stuck in the mud with it like I did yesterday. After about the third one, I came back and saw that Four was taking a break.

He's not doping today, as that wouldn't get him far with the chainsaw afterward. He is standing at the end of that forest plateau and looking through a pair of binoculars.

I walk up to him, and he offers the binoculars to me before nodding towards the mountain and sharing a comment, "I don't know who she is, but damn, she can run."

I put the binoculars over my eyes and browsed through the trees on the other side of the shore to spot the person he was talking about, but I didn't see anyone. He then pushed the binoculars in my hands to the right angle.

Okay, now, I see her.

A girl dressed in black is sprinting up into the lower layers of the trees below the mountain. Then she disappears, so I point to the fences below the area she was running from and ask, "And what's that?"

"An old military base, but it's still active. Just owned by a private company called the RF," he says, but when I keep looking that way, he pushes the binoculars out of my hands and adds, "They are very protective. Don't ever go there, and I mean, not even by accident. Many people got lost in that area, if you know what I mean."

"Are you training somewhere?" I put together slowly in their language, and now he's looking at me like I fell off Mars, so I add, "I saw you at the fight. You know how to move."

"Oh, that," he smiles. "I learned some stuff in foster care," he adds, and I smile as well because, once again, if he learned what I saw in foster care, then I am a freaking mermaid.

Chapter Twenty-One
Paige – Consequences

Damn, that's just my luck.

Today's training starts with boxing. *Of course, it does.*

I haven't even tried to wrap my hands up this morning, and now I feel every hit of the bag, cutting through the knuckles like a knife. I slowed down and took it easy for a while, but it was either too obvious, or my leader was starting to know my temper enough to see right through it.

After about fifteen minutes of slacking, he walks over to me and holds my punching bag for a while before saying, "Stop. That's enough."

I do as I was told, but I already fear something coming even before he commands, "Take your gloves off, show me your hands."

Shit. I start slowly, but even I can see the blood smudged over the top of my hands before the knuckles get fully revealed. Then, even more blood.

"Go see the medic," he commands and adds while turning away from me, "Don't come to my gym like this. Understand?" *Double shit.*

I found the medic easily, and he was just patching up my last two bloody knuckles when the leader entered the room.

"Officer," the medic said and nodded his way. No answer came from that side of the room, but I could feel the leader's presence even more than if he were screaming something loud. He stayed in the same spot next to the door until the medic was done with my hands and left the room.

I was about to get up from the chair and leave as well, but my leader's hand landed on my shoulder, and I jumped back into the seat.

He then positioned his body in front of me before saying, "This is your first strike, so I am gonna let it go, but I am sure that you know very well that fighting outside of this gym is against the rules. You can't do that, and I will not be repeating myself to you. Are we clear?"

I don't think I know anyone who would disagree with this man. However, I am still taking a breath for at least some words of an argument as I let him off too quickly last time with that Knox episode. I do not want to make that a habit, but his words stop me when coming through the damn mask again, "You were seen fighting at the scraps." *Triple shit. I've been caught.*

I nod then, and he leaves the room.

Chapter Twenty-Two

Mia – To the North

This time, Mateo picked me up earlier than usual because the race starts up north, about an hour's car ride from the lake. He talks about all kinds of stuff most of the way, but I am barely listening.

His energy is pumping with excitement almost as high as mine is. I am already in Trinity mode and can't wait to be her again. I need to get rid of my regular life for at least a few hours, shake off this weird version of myself, and shake off the guilt of the past.

Since the visit to Grandma's, all the memories are coming back to the surface again; I feel the tremble inside, the anxiety is taking over, and suddenly I can't breathe.

I will need to ask Mateo to pull over, but he is stepping on it and has over 150 kilometers per hour on the speedometer. I don't know what to do, but now, I see a shoulder coming up on the side of the road in front of us, so I am about to ask him to let me out when all of a sudden, a car flies by us. The sheer speed throws me to the door, and we are skidding sideways now.

"Oh shit," says Mateo while trying to get control of the car before we would hit the curb. I hear the screeching of the tires, and I am sure I am going to pass out now, but Mateo gets the car steady and says, "That's Four. I guess we are running behind."

I look at the car disappearing into the distance and then back at our speedometer. Mateo sees me looking at our speed while saying, "I know. He has at least 190 kilometers per hour on his meter. One day, he's gonna kill himself, that idiot."

Four. What a weird feeling. He probably hates my guts right now, and I miss him so damn much.

About two kilometers down the road, we see him at a truck stop smoking and just chilling with other racers, but we don't stop. We keep going.

We get to coordinate A, pass the security check as usual, and open the bets.

This time, I have about double the money on me than I usually have, as we expect not six but eight racers today.

And here they come.

They all buzz in peacefully, revving their engines now and then. I also see the car in the distance heading our way, which almost killed us back there.

Still, I don't feel angry. I am just somehow nervous, and I am sad.

Four is once again driving insanely fast towards us, and then he stomps on the brakes right next to where we are all standing. With the familiar screech and the smell of burning tires, he jumps out of the car. He is fuming; I can tell he's coked up higher than a kite. He shouts my way through the smoke coming out of his mouth, "Come on, Mia, cut the shit, we need to talk right now."

He then grabs my elbow, but Chris is already running our way and yelling, "Hey, hey, hey," until he gets to us and pushes Four away. Then he says more calmly, "Four, leave her alone."

"You don't know shit about us. Stay out of it," Four states but allows Chris to walk him back to his car. He then jumps in and heads over to the starting line. Chris comes back to me and says, "He's pumped up right now. I am not sure what you did to him, but if he wins, it's on you."

Meanwhile, Izzy joins us but doesn't speak until Chris moves away. Then she says, "You both need to cool it, and Four needs to keep his head in the game. Something is off with him, and he is hitting the powder too much these days. I heard he almost od'd. Chris wants me to take care of the payouts tonight. Mateo will take you home and bring you your cut later."

I nod in response. *Four almost od'd? What the hell is wrong with him? Whenever he turns into the racer, he seems to be losing control.*

"Are you ok? You look kind of off," Mateo states when he drops me off at the bottom of our hill. I force a smile, but when I get home, I realize I left both of my phones in his car. *Ugh. Crap.*

I am getting up for work in the morning, so I call it a night early, but no matter what I do, I can't fall asleep.

Oh, wait. I have the sleeping pills I got from my doctor back in the day when Grandpa died.

I take one, but it doesn't kick in fast enough, so I take some more.

Chapter Twenty-Three

Damien – Stressed Out

We are standing in the kitchen of the lake house, and I am sinking my teeth into one of the donuts the girls just pulled out of the oven. So sweet and delicious.

"I don't know what's gonna happen," Rob says and hops up to sit on the counter. Adele comes over to him to ask, "What's wrong?"

"Well, Grandma was just being stupid, and I think Mia is taking it badly. You should have seen the ride home. It was horrible to see Mia sad like that."

Adele hugs him and adds, "It's all gonna be okay, don't worry."

"I dunno about that," he shakes his head. Then he continues about how angry he is with Grandma and that he will not go to visit her again until she gets her shit together, but then his phone rings, interrupting him. He listens briefly before yelling, "Shit! I am on my way. I'll be there as soon as I can."

With that, he turns to David, looking shaken up. "That was Four. Mia tried to attempt suicide. She took some pills."

"Go, go! Get out of here!" Adele shouts, and at the same time, I hear the EMT siren somewhere in the distance. When we get to our house, Four and his ambulance are already gone, and the family is about to lock the door and leave as well.

I jump into the car with them, and we head towards the hospital, but the nurses don't let us see Mia anyway when we get there. They also don't say a damn thing about how she is doing. We just sit and wait in one of the emptiest waiting rooms you can imagine.

We spot Mia quickly before the door closes behind one of the nurses. She doesn't look the best, but her monitor is beeping, so at least that's a good sign.

Finally, a while later, the doctor came over to us and said Mia was going to be okay, which was amazing. Then he asked all of us who saw her eat last, and we just looked blankly at each other. With that, he left.

The look on my dad's face after the doctor walked away was too painful to watch. I have never seen him this way before. Completely broken. My chest starts pounding, and I just can't be part of this, so I get up and go outside for at least a few minutes. I need some air.

Rob comes out as well after a few minutes, lays down on his back in the grass by one of the pillars at the entrance, and covers his eyes with his hand. I feel alone like never before.

After another ten or fifteen minutes, Anna appears in the doorway and says, "Guys, we can go in to see her."

Rob puts his hands behind his back, and the kick-up move gets him from lying on his back to standing on his feet in one motion. *Dope.*

When we get to Mia's room, she is still out cold, and the doctor is standing there with a clipboard, looking suspicious.

He starts asking about Mia and what support she is getting for her Anxiety and PTSD, and he lists a few other things I haven't heard about before. Once he is done, Anna says the family has no concerns. *Really? I do. Can she not see there is something weird about this girl?*

I guess the doctor feels the same way as I do. He points to the other side of the bed and asks, "Well, what do you think these are? They must be self-inflicted."

We all follow his gaze over to Mia. The whole side of her leg has a bunch of cuts of all sizes.

What the hell! Is she cutting herself?

Then the doctor speaks again. "We'll have to run a psychology test and keep her in for an observation for the time being. We cannot send her home in this state; she could try to harm herself again."

"No, they are not self-inflicted!" Four blurts out, and we all look in his direction at the same time. "It was an accident. We didn't see the glass and went through it. I have the same cuts, see?"

With that, he lifts his shorts up a bit. His thigh has the same type of cuts, plus a big older one in the middle that is stitched up.

There we go. That's what must have made him limp for days.

The doctor nods and says, "Then, we'll just have to see what happened with the medication misuse. We need her side of the story."

Rob turns around and walks out of the room without another word.

Four follows behind him, and then it comes to me. The night Four told us about the great sex he had and about falling through the glass, all of it.

It was with her. Mia? Rob is going to kill him. Although, I hope that Four won't fight back, as I don't think anyone would want to see those two in a real fight. That wouldn't be good.

I'm sure I can't help with anything, but I am rushing out of the room after them anyway.

I get outside just when Rob pushes Four into the pillar that he was lying next to a few minutes ago, with a voice that is just livid, "Are you fucking kidding me right now? Mia? Seriously? You were talking about her the other day?"

With that, Rob starts pacing back and forth while rubbing his forehead.

"It's not like that, I swear," Four gestures and tries to follow him, but Rob shoves his chest, sending him towards the pillar, and holds him there while saying, "I don't give a flying fuck about your body count, you will stay away from her!"

"I can't do that," says Four, and now I am sure he has a death wish. After the next hit, he stopped breathing for a bit but tried to cough it out, stating, "It doesn't matter what you do, mate; if she wants me, then she wants me."

Rob spreads his arms and shakes his head in disbelief again. "What the hell is wrong with you? This is Mia we're talking about!"

"Exactly," Four coughs out, but Rob only lifts his hand and says, "You know what? Just go. Get the fuck out of here! I can't deal with you right now."

Chapter Twenty-Four
Mia – The Room That I Know

Well, this dream sucks.

I am in an ambulance, and there is a needle pulsing in my arm, plus this weird flutter around my body is now changing into the sound of drums going in my head at regular intervals. And it's not like I wouldn't notice the medic's mouth moving in front of my eyes, but the sound of the siren is coming in first and takes all the space of my attention. *Exhausted. I am dropping out of this. Get me out.*

Then I feel more peaceful and force my eyes open again.

Wait. I recognize this room. I have been here so many times.

The guy at the bottom of my bed smiles and says, "Well, hello there, Mia, welcome back. We are happy you're finally awake."

He is a doctor, and I know him. I have been on his shifts as well. He starts talking, and I get all the facts now.

This is not a dream. I overdid it with the sleeping pills. Shit.

I know the drill, so I nod to everything he proposes so they won't detain me here too long.

He then tells me my family left a while ago, but a guy at the front is waiting for me to wake up. I nod when he asks me if he can send him in.

It must be Four.

My body shivers now, and I can't wait to see him.

"Dope having you back," sounds from the door a second later, and Rob's body of muscles walks in.

His aura is dark lava red, pumping like he is ready to kill somebody. Why is he so angry?

"Oh, thank God, she is awake," says Mom while walking in right behind him.

Rob moves over to the window and stares through it while tapping on the left side of the glass. "There is an empty parking spot right over there. He's freaking blind."

Mom smiles and explains, "We went home for more of your stuff. Dad is parking the car now, but he will bring it. I took what was in the dryer, the shorts you wear all the time."

I nod, and she comes closer to ask, "How are you feeling?"

Oh crap, she looks exhausted.

"I am fine," I say but grab the edge of the bed anxiously. Then Rob responds from the window, "Then explain it to the doctor, and you can go home."

"You shouldn't have to stay here more than a week," Mom adds innocently, but she shows how stressed she feels by unnecessarily tucking in the corners of my bed. *Mom, it's useless to try lying to me. I can feel your energy.*

I look up and ask, "A whole week?"

"At least," Dad drops out while walking through the door and getting a threatening look from Mom before she turns back to me with another attempt. "There are some tests to do. The usual, you know?"

"Tests?" I ask into the room, but they only look at each other and give me no answer.

"What tests?" I ask, but Dad turns his face to my monitors, and Mom starts washing her hands in the sink by the wall. Hence, the only option is to go for the only person with truthful energy in this room.

"Rob?" I called out, and he fired back, as expected. "You have some psychological issues, plus you are anorexic, and that's what's up. All right?"

"Oh, no one thinks you're anorexic," Mom tries her low-key energy of lies again and sends another of her looks over to him, but Rob shakes his head. "That's cap. Don't bullshit her."

"Please," she shushes him, looking back at me to deliver as

gently as possible. "It's just some stupid tests, nothing more."

"Rob?" I turn to him again for the truth.

He smiles triumphantly and comes over to my side. "No one remembers the last time you grabbed a bite. Plus, you and I have other shit to talk about once they are all out of here."

I hate his superiority over me right now.

Mom comes and strokes my head. "Don't worry, everything is going to be okay." *Well, that story is cap for sure.*

At that point, I kind of froze, staring at the ceiling. I zoned out a bit, I guess.

"Be nice to her!" I then heard Mom telling Rob when they were on their way out.

Rob turns from the door the second it shuts behind them, but he only stands there, looking my way. He doesn't say anything because he knows he doesn't have to.

I feel the spike in his energy. Shit.

Then he finally takes a deep breath and says, "First, I said that you going to Grandma's was the dumbest idea ever, but why would they listen to me, right? That's that, but second, not that's any of my business, but you slept with Four. What the fuck is wrong with you?"

Oh, no.

"He told you that?"

He looks back at me, and his aura is now literally of a carmine color before he says, "Don't even go there, Mia, don't you dare."

"Rob," I try calmly, but he jumps right into it. "Don't "Rob" me right now! Are you out of your mind? He is a junkie, and you know that because you used coke with him. Are you for real? Do you want to get hooked on it as well? Is that what this is all about?"

I shake my head as much as I can, but I see he is now behind the point of no return. He is on a power play, and the only thing you can do is stay out of his way.

Chapter Twenty-Five
Damien – The Phone

Oh damn, this is awkward.

Neither Rob nor Four speaks to each other, and we are all somewhere in between the two of them.

Four then offers to pick up goods from the warehouse, and I am pushed into the car with him. *He is tired and looks like shit.*

"Are you okay?" is the only question that comes to my mind and the only thing I can really say right now.

He keeps his electric eyes on the road when saying, "How can I sum it up for you, little buddy. Well, Rob doesn't want me near Mia, period, and the thing is, I don't even know if she gives a fuck. Not a single message back from her, nothing. So, I have no idea what to do with that."

I don't say anything back because who knows what to say at this point.

We then get the goods at the warehouse and are on our way back when his phone starts ringing. When he taps on the answer button, the sound goes straight to the car speakers.

"Hey," says the guy on the other end. "You owe me, bro."

Four replies, "I am good for it; what is it?"

"I made Chris move the date as you wanted. Are you coming to the poker game tonight? Are you playing?"

"You bet I am," Four replies with a tone finishing the conversation, but the guy comes back with, "Oh, one more thing. Where are you now?"

Four answers, "Leaving the Coop, why?"

"Wait there. I'll meet you in five."

"K, I'll be here," Four says, then he pulls over, and we wait.

The guy who shows up drives a crazy-colored car and wears rapper-style clothes. His name is Mateo.

He talks to Four for a while, then gives him something and nods my way when leaving. Four then lands his ass back into the car.

"It's your time to help, little buddy," he informs and seems to be in a much better mood all of a sudden.

He then gives me a cell phone. I look at it and say, "If you haven't heard yet, my name is Damien, and what am I to do with this?"

Four takes a deep breath before saying, "Listen to me. I need you to be smart about this, so try really hard, okay?"

Does he really think I am an idiot, or is he just kidding right now?

Then he adds, "This is Mia's phone. I need you to hide it in the house, but not too well and not too obvious either. Got it?"

I better be honest. "No, I don't get it."

"Yeah, shocker," he smirked and added very slowly, "The phone needs to be found around the house, but they need to think they overlooked it at first, not that it had been brought to the house now. Got it?"

No, I still don't understand the game, but I can't say that to him again.

Rob is already waiting outside when we get to the Trap. He immediately takes the boxes out of the car and growls, "Next time, I'll walk over there. It'll be here faster."

Four shakes his head to signal me not to say anything.

I wasn't going to. I don't have a death wish.

Chapter Twenty-Six

Mia – The Visits

And here I am.

With a blanket pulled over my head, I am trying to sort out the memories of my past until I am left with a harsh reality.

Left with that moment when I stopped being a neurotypical girl. The moment my world lost its regular colors and turned into an all-over-stabbing depression stronger than any of the voices in my head before.

And amid this misery, a door opens.

"Hey," Rob says, automatically taking over the entire room without realizing it.

He wrinkles his nose. "Well, it sure stinks in here. Did they just pour bleach all over the floor or something? If Four didn't kill you by driving you here, the stink of this definitely will," he then howls behind his back. "Can you prop the door open, or we are all going to choke to death in here."

"Hi," comes from that direction of the door, and Adele enters with a gentle, calming smile.

That's when Rob points at my bedside table covered with aging fruit and says, "Did I call it or what?"

"Anna wanted us to bring you more fruit. Obviously, not a good idea," Adele explains, pulling a chipped chess piece from her pocket and tossing it onto my blanket.

It is a good luck charm that I gave to Four when he was going for his appendectomy surgery. I wanted to tell her to thank him, but before I could say anything, Rob jumped in with a comment, "Ah, nice, but a piece of fried chicken would probably help her more right now, don't you think?"

He is turning away from me, so I grab one of the dying oranges and throw it in his direction. Somehow, like always, he catches it. That's a hockey thing, I guess.

Then they start talking about Trap. They didn't expect anything from me, so I successfully endured the rest of their visit.

After they leave, I pull the covers over my head and try not to breathe. It doesn't work very well.

I then force myself to get up, walk into the common area, where the TV is, and start watching the news.

NHL highlights are showing right now and remind me of home. *Sadness.*

Rob was still pissed when he left earlier. Not giving me a chance to keep Four in my life other than as a very distant friend.

That is far from what I want.

"You have a visitor, Mia," I hear from the doorway and turn to look.

The head nurse stands there and says, "A boy is coming for a visit. I will allow it only because it's you, you know that. Visiting hours are over. Go take a peek quickly if you want to see him."

And I did just that.

From behind her, I see somebody's back. It is Four with his motorcycle gear on. It's him, it's really him. She looks at me; I nod, walking through the door and taking a deep breath because he just took it away from me completely with a single look.

He is so hot. Even the way he moves gets any girl going.

"Hey," he smiles. *Damn that smile.*

He says, "I am sorry; I know it's late, but I had to see you."

At first glance, it's nice that he is not pumping at his usual coked-up level. He is clean, but there is a vibe of nervousness within him that I have never felt in his body before.

I am walking over to him, but my gaze stops on the stretcher being pulled out of the ambulance that just arrived at the front door of the next building.

The medics are running towards the emergency, red in the face and pumping with a desperate energy flow. Still, the aura around the body on the stretcher is almost undetectable.

A swell of sadness comes over me. I approach and touch the glass window before me as if I could grasp the last flutter of that disappearing vibration. Then I feel the strong wave of Four's energy behind me even before he asks, "Are you okay? Do you want me to go? Should I not have come?"

I looked at him, and at that moment, another flood of feelings hit me straight on, and all was now clear as a day. *No, I don't want you to leave. Ever.*

I take the two steps of the space left between us, and his lips are on mine.

Maybe he started kissing me, or it was the other way around, who cares. I belong with him, and he belongs with me. *Facts.*

He then pulls back away from me and says as he goes to sit down, "Rob gave me an ultimatum."

I nod and say, "Same here."

"What are we going to do then?"

Chapter Twenty-Seven

Paige - A Poker Night

Carly invited me to the city for lunch. I usually refuse as she likes to wear the most expensive clothes from head to toe, and people stare at us a bit too much. Still, today, I need a distraction, so why not.

We got some shopping done and then ate in one of the most expensive restaurants in the city. Overall, we had a good time together, but if I hear Rob's name mentioned one more time today, I might actually end somebody. Carly is head over heels in love with him and hasn't stopped talking about him for the last three hours straight. It is getting a bit much, to say the least.

She also bought super fancy lingerie as Rob is coming into the club tonight. She persuaded me to buy some as well.

At the restaurant, Carly pointed out that guys sitting in the corner were checking me out, but I was not looking to get involved with anyone.

I have only slept with men twice in my life. I was young, and both times were taken against my will. Even that tiny mental reminder of it makes my chest rip open again. I remember the feeling of lying there naked in pain, but even then, I wasn't angry at the guy as much as I was angry at myself. As if I was the one who allowed that to happen to me.

When I turned fourteen and was homeless at the time, the RF agency scouts came around. I was the first to sign up for the training camp. With so many girls trying to get in, only three spots were available then, but I knew I had to make it.

I trained harder than anyone. The vision of someone using my body again drove me to the edge, and it still does.

Carly says that Rob always leaves her satisfied sexually. He is among the most handsome guys I've ever seen. Still, even with someone as handsome as him, I can't imagine the act of intercourse being somehow nice after what I have been through.

Now, in the eyes of the outside world, I am just a bartender and can do whatever I want. I won that freedom by passing the first three training levels at the base. Compensation for the years of sweat, blood, pain, tears and denial.

Tonight, the bar is packed full, and I am enjoying myself. I like to keep my mind and hands busy all the time. The hockey game is running on the TV behind me, and Carly won't move her eyes off the screen for a second when Rob is on the ice. It makes me smile.

I prepared a tray of drinks and took it downstairs to the private card room. I tried not to disturb the players, as I was told they were playing poker for a big load of money, but when I got there, they were not playing quite yet.

They are just talking amongst each other. I am not really listening to their conversation; I am just organizing the bar, so I don't have to return down again while they are playing.

Still, I hear the guy in the blue suit asking the man sitting beside him. "Where the heck is he? Dex, did you call him?"

Dex answers him with a question, "Who? Four? Don't worry; he'll be here soon."

The blue-suit man continues nervously, "He's probably drowning in some pussy and forgot about the game. I heard how many chicks he turns down daily; that lucky son of a bitch, eh?"

Dex sits there calmly counting his chips and then replies, "Well, people say a lot of things, but have you actually heard a girl saying that they slept together? I don't think he has anything going on. People just like to make shit up sometimes for something to talk about."

"Well, I'll ask him if he's ever gonna get here. Damn it, where is he?"

With that, I closed the door and stepped into the elevator, which took me back upstairs.

I get behind the main bar and see Carly cracked under pressure. She now has two lines of white powder waiting on the bar in front of her. I have never seen her do drugs in public like this, and

I am interested to see who she is waiting to do them with, but first, I have to get the drink for the guy who just ordered.

It's a quick gin and tonic, and I am just turning back with it when I see that Carly's friend has arrived. I move closer to look at him, but he has already bent down to snort his line, so I can't tell if I have seen him before. After that, he quickly lifts his head back up, and his eyes meet mine. I stay frozen for a moment. Just staring at him as he is unimaginable. Flawless.

His face, his body, his piercing azure eyes. I mean, what is this? Is he even human?

Carly wipes her nose and then gestures between us while saying, "Four, this is Paige. Paige, this is Four."

I nod and manage to get out "Hi" while letting the deep of his eyes to sink into mine. *Shit.*

Wait. He could be a test. The RF could have sent him to see if I would go off the track. Well, they couldn't find anyone better than this. Fuck, he is hot.

I snap my gaze away, and then I quickly move to the other side of the bar and deliver the drink order while trying not to look at Four again.

Though, is there even a way not to look at him?

Damn. I have never been attracted to anyone like this.

Four is a tall guy. His muscular body is covered with caramel toned skin, and he moves the way primed just about for anything. The beauty of his face is simply beyond extraordinary, and I can't take my eyes off him. The strong jawline, perfectly toned cheeks, and piercing eyes drew me in without even trying. *Shit. If this was a test, I most definitely bombed it.*

My gaze follows him as he leaves for the elevator. He must be the one the other poker players were waiting for downstairs. He must not have been a test then. *Phew.*

When I return, Carly is back to watching the game, but she must have spotted my eyes on him as she says, "He is a racer. Hence the alias. Four."

"What is his actual name?" I ask curiously.

Carly looks back at me, surprised by the question. "Who gives a shit? Everyone calls him Four. But stay clear of him."

I react faster than I want to admit when I ask, "Why?"

"He's not for a girl like you. Trust me, he is an animal and a player for sure. He is into cars, booze, drugs, you name it."

Tracy walks up to her quickly, "Who is? What are we talking about?"

Carly puts on her *"I like to sound interesting face"* and says, "Paige was asking about Four."

Tracy bursts out laughing, "What? Four and the virgin over here? He would split her in half."

They both giggle before Carly turns back to me and adds, "You see? As I told you, he means real heat and real danger. You got it?"

Oh, I got it, but they don't need to worry about it. As handsome as he is, I am sure not getting close to him. Ever.

Chapter Twenty-Eight

Damien – A Real Talk

The sun is getting in through the blinds and finds my eyes. All right, all right, I am getting up.

I turn my phone over to check the time. *Damn. I hope Rob slept here and not over at his place, as I need a ride. No one could force me to walk all the way over to the lake.*

I drag my body to his old room and then move around in the darkness until I get to where I think his bed is.

I shove the body lying there with full strength, but what I get is a girl's voice under my hand. "What?"

I jump back, but she is already speaking in the other direction. "Rob, we must've slept in!"

At that, the body next to her moves, the blinds hum, and there is light filling the room. Rob starts looking through the mess on the floor for some clothes. I am heading out.

He catches up with me at the tennis courts.

"I am exhausted," he says, but he sure doesn't look like it. I know he can run a six-minute mile without breaking a sweat, but I am confused. It seems like he actually wants to speak to me. *Well, that's a first.*

"She came by the midnight train. It was a tough night. I had to get it out of my system, if you know what I mean. Plus, you have to give back to the fans, right? Ask coach Rudy." He smiles, and I am trying to act like Four would. *Like whatever.*

"Dope," I say, as I am sure that's good enough.

"Yeah, you don't need to be coked up to your eyeballs to have a good time, am I right?"

Do I wanna start him off? Why not, but I am done with this crap. I am speaking in English.

"You are still pissed with Four? You think he'll hurt Mia?"

"Nah, he won't because he can't," he returns in English and runs his hand through his hair before adding, "I have never asked her straight on, but I am sure she can actually read minds or something of that sort. She would see it coming before his stupid head even thought of it."

Oh, that's why she never speaks to me. I call her bad shit crazy in my head about ten times a day.

"Oh," I say aloud, and he turns to me with a question, "Something is adding up?"

I confirm, "It sure is."

He then continues, "And Four? He is a lot of things with a lot of covers, but he is not a liar. He told me he didn't get her any drugs, and I believe him. She was already high when they met, and he thought she was somebody else. Do you remember that?"

I nod. "Yes, he thought she was some Trinity, so what now?"

"Well, now it better be absolutely nothing. Plus, I heard he landed a good hand in poker last night, so he'll be in a good mood today, and we can all move on from this."

Chapter Twenty-Nine

Mia – Going to the Movies

I said that I was going to the movies. It made Mom so happy and me so guilty for lying to her that I ate almost half of the ridiculous portion of food she forced on my plate.

It was too much, and I will be sick for sure, but at least with that, I am officially allowed to leave. I am taking Dad's car, which has tracking, so I must park it at the theatre parking lot.

Mateo asked alias Six, one of the racers, to get me on his way and drive me to the race. Six was already waiting for me in the parking lot when I arrived. I got into his car, and we set off.

I can read his energy and feel that he's watching me as well. Then, he starts some small talk, but I am too much in my head for that.

The road picked for tonight is dope. Not a single hill in site. It is just a flat, long stretch of pavement as far as the eye can see. Every racer's dream.

We are expecting eight cars again tonight.

"Mateo said you came with Six. Oh girl, you move fast," drops Izzy my way when she brings me the laptop. I open it and find a little bag of white powder on the keyboard. She winks at me and says, "Just in case you want it."

I look up at her, wanting to give it back, but she shakes her head and bites her bottom lip when confessing, "Damn, I've missed you."

With that, she turns and walks away.

I am watching the starting line nervously as I plan to speak to Four before the race begins.

There. Finally, here he comes.

But he is moving slowly this time, and I am about to take the first step toward him when I spot the inside of his car through the pulled-down windows. Tracy is sitting in the passenger seat, leaning over the center console. *In front of everybody? Is he for real? Is he getting sucked off right here right now?*

"Yeah, sorry about that," says Mateo, who shows up beside me. "I guess that's a payback as I told him you are here with Six."

"Whatever makes him happy," I hear myself saying, but I know he is not.

I can read him. I can feel his energy. He is high on something, angry, and somehow confused. I know that right after he snaps back out of the orgasm that he is about to have, he will know it as well.

Shit. I forgot what time it was. The movie will be over in nine minutes.

I will grab Mateo's car and leave it for him at the theatre as agreed, but now, I have to step on it.

I am going 160 kilometers per hour most of the way, and the clock is ticking. I am racing between the cars on the highway as fast as I can, but when I get closer to the city, I realize I have someone on my tail. *Oh no, is it the cops?*

I pull into the next gas station, and the car follows me. I keep checking my rear-view mirror, but in the end, it's only Chris. *Phew.*

He pulls over next to me and rolls down his window before yelling over the music playing in his car.

"Hey, next time, I am grabbing a car for you to race. Geez, the way you drive, I thought you were Four. Damn."

Chapter Thirty

Paige – A Race Night Out

My shift was over, but when I was walking to my car, I noticed one of the elders from our agency waiting in the back alley behind the bar. He waved at me and then pointed to his car, so I walked over and got in. I hoped this meeting was about my assignment, but it wasn't. He just needed me for a company event. *Sigh.*

He tells me to call him Ronnie and asks me to leave my phone behind. That's not a problem, as I don't have it on me anyway.

I plan to speak to him on the way and get some info about a possible assignment for me, but within five or so minutes of the ride, he picks up another two girls. Tracy and Stef. I know them both. They are sleeping with guys for money, and even though they spend a lot of time in the bar, they are on their own.

Ronnie drives for about twenty minutes and then stops near a lonely-looking intersection. The plan is for Tracy and Stef to stay here while I go with Ronnie to the city. Then the plans change as he receives a text and turns towards me to say, "You are going with them."

Okay. I was hoping to go into the city, take a shower at my place, and change clothes, but whatever. I guess I don't have a say in this.

I got out of the car and leaned over to fix my skirt quickly when a car flew by me so fast, almost hitting the open door. *Damned racers.*

"Oh, that's Four. I hope to get my hands on him tonight," says Tracy, but Stef yells at the same time. "I got it. I have the coordinates."

"Did you pay?" comes from Ronnie through the open window of the car.

"Yes," she answers quickly, but he adds, "Then double it and leave your phones with me. All of you."

After that, he gave us a map and a pen and asked me to mark the longitude and latitude on it.

He then hands me a black baseball cap and a bandana while apologizing, "Girls wear wigs and sunglasses in there, but I have only this in my car. Please, put it on."

I wrap the bandana around the bottom of my face, let my hair run down over it, and put on the baseball cap. I actually look pretty good in it. Only I wish that I had the sunglasses. My green eyes tend to give me away when I am to be disguised.

Soon after I am done with that, another car pulls in. The driver gets out and throws the car keys to Tracy. She starts walking toward the vehicle, practically singing, "Get the map and get in, girls; I am driving!"

Hold on there, precious. I don't like to be told what to do, especially not by a bimbo like you. Don't push it.

And on top of it all, she drives like an idiot. *Sigh.*

After a while, she finally pulls over, and we get out of the car, but where are we, and what the heck is going on here?

We are walking towards a lineup of people. It looks like some sort of security check. One of them is a woman who moves towards me and starts patting down my body.

Wow, careful there, sweetheart. You are walking a fine line here.

After the check, we walk through a gate into some sort of a complex. I immediately start checking out my surroundings for an escape route.

The fence is a regular six-foot fence. It's easy enough to get over; I've jumped many of those in training before.

However, the people at the front would be tricky to go through if I needed to get out. I would probably aim for the man on the right side with the big gut or maybe for the woman, who looks rather weak. She also exposed herself while searching me so I know that I can take her.

Now we are walking along some old factory walls, and I start hearing music, revving car engines, and people. A lot of people. This must be the car race everyone has been talking about.

Stef and Tracy are super excited and instantly move to the front of the line.

I have no idea what I am to do here. I just observe and memorize my surroundings for now. I passed the T Maze test at the base with flying colors, so why not? But after a while, I thought I should at least move away from Tracy and Stef as I didn't want anyone thinking I was one of them and try to buy me for the night.

If anyone tried that, it would be their last one.

I began to move away, but at the exact moment, a car stopped right in front of Tracy and me. The door flies open, and a deep voice booms inside the vehicle, commanding, "Tracy, get in."

His tone makes me jump back a bit, and I peer inside.

Of course, it is the one and only. It's Four.

Like every man here tonight, he is wearing a mask that shows only his eyes and lips, but there are no other eyes like this.

He is looking back at me now, his intense stare scanning me up and down, but I am not one to yield, so I glare back just the same. Even though staying calm under his gaze is not easy, my eyes don't move. Not even when I catch the car keys that Tracy throws my way from the side. *Shit. I can't believe I caught it. I better be careful. There is no point in getting my cover blown over this.*

It is a delayed reaction, but I still drop the keys on the ground. The corner of his lip turns up a bit into a smirk. *I guess he thinks that I am clumsy. That's fine, better than him finding out I am trained.*

Then Tracy interrupts my stare when she walks over to me anyway and whispers, "He never goes for more than a blow job, so tell Stef I'll text her when I am done with him."

"You go ahead and have fun with that crackhead," I say back to her and hope that he can read lips because I would love to send him a message. His arrogance seems to be begging for it.

Tracy then jumped into his car, and at that point, the crowd started moving in the direction of the starting line, so I also walked that way.

"Hey, you need a ride?" comes from the window of a car slowly passing me by.

"I think I am good," I answer at first, but then I look at the guy again as he takes his mask off. I like his hair, and his eyes have a pleasant and friendly smile within them, so why not.

I slide into the seat next to him, and he sticks his knuckles towards me for a fist bump. Then he says, "My name is Con. Alias Three. What's your name?"

"Paige," I respond and bump his waiting knuckles.

"It's gonna be a wild race today," he says while we start moving, and he kind of sniffles at the same time.

I ask, "What's so wild about today?"

"More bones in the pot than usual, you know?" he smiles back before changing his facial expression and adding seriously. "You will probably go nuts for Four, eh?" He points toward the car in front of us before he turns back to me with, "All the girls always do, but before that, I want you to know that you have other options."

He is clearly trying to hit on me.

"Thanks," I answer shyer than I planned on sounding, but then I quickly think of a lie, "I am actually into girls more."

"Yo, the last one who said that was then rolling in the glass with him in front of everybody, so I'd keep that to yourself because he likes the challenge, you know? Four is my buddy and all, but also an arrogant son of a bitch when it comes to chicks."

Now, it's up to me to share a smile and say, "Thanks for the heads up."

"Well, you gonna need it," he finishes up and points his index finger to Four's right mirror, through which he is looking directly back at me.

"Don't worry. He just doesn't do it for me," I say firmly. With that, he stops, and I am getting out of the car.

"Let's have a drink on that at the party," he sends after me; I nod back towards him while he puts his mask back on.

Chapter Thirty-One

Paige – The After-Party

It's a shame that Con didn't win the race.

He came in second, right behind Four, all because he didn't want to fly through the bushes blindly like Four did, which cost him the win.

After the payouts, Con picked me up, and we are now heading to the after-party. The coordinates took us to a large, empty warehouse, which, I guess, is the venue for tonight.

Con brings me a drink before I even have a chance to ask for it, which I appreciate, but if I were to get one for myself, I would have gotten something else; beer is not my favorite.

We are sitting on the floor together in the corner of the room and chatting for a bit. He grabs and holds onto my hand. He then spots Four's eyes on us and comments, "I like nothing more than see him tripping. He really likes you or doesn't, which is even better."

I didn't say anything and didn't look Four's way either. Still, Con was having a good time, knowing that, for whatever reason, Four was irritated by me, him, or the both of us together.

Tracy came to us at some point and offered a joint. Con took it from her, and I inhaled the smoke from him while ignoring Four's voice that came from somewhere behind Tracy, stating, "Yeah, you should knock yourself out."

Con then went to the bar to get us another drink and asked me when he returned, "You and Four. Do you guys know each other or something?"

I thought out loud, "Well, I only know his name, but that's about it."

Con continues, "You see, he seems genuinely worried about me. Not you, but me. Can you believe it? Like, if I do you wrong, you will leave me dead in the ditch or something, you know?"

I smiled. "A ditch? Don't worry. That's not my thing for a first date-kill. Plus, I am into girls, remember?"

"Oh, I forgot about that," he admits but seems to be breathing easier.

I, on the other hand, am worried. Four is up to something.

Around five in the morning, I realized there weren't many people left at the party, so I decided to call it a night. Con was in no shape to get behind the wheel with all the drinks he had, so I grabbed the keys and offered to drive his car. He agreed, so we started to walk towards it.

I overheard Tracy yelling something behind us to Four, but I ignored her and kept walking.

We got on the road after a couple of minutes, and I didn't even realize how fast I was going until I turned my head and noticed

Four's car racing beside us. The trees, houses, and signs around disappearing made me look at the meter. Wow, 170 kilometers per hour. *Shit, I should really slow down.*

"Too late to back out of it now," says Con, who is lying on the passenger's seat drunkenly. He ripped his mask off, and I saw him flipping Four off through the window.

Four's revving engine comes as a response to the middle finger, so I decide to step on it. Four jumps at the opportunity, and before I know it, we are racing. The heavy trucks moving slowly throughout the night complicate things.

I was flying between them but almost crashed into the curb twice, and I spotted Four's cocky looking. That makes me step on the gas even more.

You arrogant bastard. I can do this as well, you know.

But then we got on the open road away from the traffic of other cars, and I took my words back as he passed me going more than 180 kilometers per hour. He is most definitely crazy and also probably coked up out of his mind, so there is no way I will attempt to win against this idiot. I waited for him to disappear into the distance and take the next exit.

Chapter Thirty-Two

Mia – I am in

"Four," Mateo says when I ask who won the race. I roll my eyes; he gives me my cut and smiles. "He was pumped. Tracy must have thrown a mean one before the race."

With that, he realized he was speaking to me and added, "Shoot, sorry, I probably shouldn't have said that."

I shake my head like it's okay, and he says, "It's good that he won. He owed money for moving the date for you."

"For me?"

"Yes, he said you were at the hospital and couldn't make it, so he had the race moved a week. I then met him in the city and gave him both your phones."

Oh, he gave him both phones: the one that Four brought me to the hospital and also the other one that our mom found in my bathrobe pocket, where I would never put it.

He interrupts my thoughts with a question, "How is Six?"

"He's okay, I think," I say, confused, before adding, "but I heard he crashed, and I don't think he's riding any time soon."

"Well, he doesn't have to. Chris has you on the list now," he says, and before I start laughing, he adds, "I have never seen so many bets on a girl before."

He then looks at me again and says, "It's a shame you couldn't stay after the race. They all wanted to party with you. Even Izzy can't get you out of her head. They all owe me. I was the one who found you."

I smile and get out of the car, but after he leaves, I grab my phone and text Chris immediately to take me off the list.

He is okay with it as far as the depth goes back on Four.

No, I don't want that. I don't want Four paying to do me a favor.

I start typing again. "Okay, sign me up then."

Chapter Thirty-Three

Damien – A Bus Party

Four helps me to throw another log and then says, "I hope you are down for chicks and booze tonight because we are gonna get fucked up."

"What?" I ask happily, and he continues, "We are gonna chill with the hockey players. They have six wins in a row, so it'll be big. Plus, I am itching for a girl. I haven't had one since Tuesday."

I need to point it out, so I say, "Tuesday was yesterday, wasn't it?"

"Exactly, that's my point. Let's head over to Steve's Bar. I wanna get loose, and I want Paige to be there. I don't know what game she thinks she's playing, but she needs to know that I don't give a shit."

I don't think that's the way to do it, dude, but whatever.

The bus with the hockey players showed up around eleven at night. Four and I were the last ones to get on board. I noticed all the girls on the bus were already wasted and barely dressed at that point; plus, there was so much booze in there that it was crazy.

One of the girls, Tracy, had obviously been waiting there for Four. I got the attention of her sidekick, Stef, and it didn't take me long to get completely lost in her. Rob's voice snapped me out of it when he said, "Hey, bro, hit me with another one."

I looked up, but he was actually showing his empty beer bottle to Four, who was walking towards the front of the bus.

Others quickly jumped on the chance of another drink, which made Four hand out a couple of beers and other drinks before he finally growled back, "You should have brought the bartender for this."

Tracy replied, "Oh, Paige? She's not working tonight, and she is not fun anyway. Plus, she definitely wouldn't come near you."

He handed me a bottle of vodka while turning back to her and asking, "Why?"

"First, we told her not to. Second, she wouldn't anyway. She is weird. She is not dating girls, but she is not dating guys either. She doesn't seem to want to date anyone."

"Oh, no," comes from Rob with a smile, "Don't say that in front of Four. He'll take on the challenge."

"She's not my type anyway, so whatever," says Four, making Rob shake his head. "Great. A week with Mia, and he has a type now, apparently."

Tracy wraps her arms around Four as if trying to stand up for him when she says, "Well, I am his type, though, right?"

"Sure, why not," replies Four, "If you are okay having fun with the crackhead like me."

"Wow, did you hear Paige say that?" Tracy squeals back, but Four smiles and says, "Don't worry about it."

Then they returned to their seats, and we saw more of Four than we ever wanted. Somewhere between them having fun, Four whistles over at Rob, sitting a couple of seats in front of him, and points out of the window, asking, "Did you see that?"

I also looked where Four was pointing and saw some crazy person jumping off the cliff.

Rob nods and turns back to Four, with his face lightened by interest, when he asks, "A cliff dive is impossible from up there, isn't it?"

"It's a wingsuit base jump," Four judges almost jealously while still looking that way and adding, "But from that spot, it's nuts. I need to find out who that is and speak to the idiot."

Chapter Thirty-Four

Mia – A Ride Home

My shift is finally over.

I made it to the bus stop on time and was now looking for the bus card when my eyes wandered across the street. Four was standing there, leaning against the door of his car and looking down at his phone. A text from him lit up on mine at the exact moment he looked up at me and smiled. I started walking over towards him. He then opened the passenger door for me, but I stopped.

Why should I have anything to do with you?

"Hope in," he says, but I am just looking into his eyes, not moving a step more.

Though, I wish it would be easier. Why do I want to touch him so much?

He smiles as if he would know, keeps looking back, and gently separates the words for me when saying, "Mia. Please. Get in the car."

Oh shit. Look at his lips. Okay. I'll just do it.

After I hop in, he turns the car on, and we head off. I guess he is driving me home. His energy hit me, and I started to read him. *Wow, that is interesting. He is sober, and he is nervous or maybe excited. I remember this pumping and flowing of his energy. The same as when he bought his bike last summer and the same when he was taking my clothes off a few days ago. Damn. The heat in my face again. Focus!*

"I need you to step down from the race," he says with a serious tone behind his words, and with that, my daydream is definitely over. *So, stop staring at him!*

There, I feel a spike of urgency within him. *He worries about me.*

"Con, alias Three, will never have you win. It's not personal. He just won't allow a girl to win any race. He will crash into you, injure you; he'll do anything. You need to get out."

I shake my head and admit, "It's too late. I can't."

"Okay, then you must stay behind and watch your mirrors," Four adds. He is now racing between the cars around us on the road so fast that it makes me grip the seat belt and look over at him. I feel the tremble within him even before he says, "If anything happens to you, I swear I don't know what I would do, Mia."

His knuckles are going white from grabbing hold of the steering wheel so tightly, so I reach over to him, and my left hand touches his elbow. I shiver but also feel a spike in his energy again.

He then pulled over so fast that we almost ran into the ditch.

I try not to stare at him, but it's virtually impossible. I feel stupid, but the question comes out on its own. "Did you sleep with Tracy?"

"No," he responds right away. "I don't sleep around, but I am hardly a one-girl kind of guy either, you know me."

Then he rubs his hair a bit. "I know you are with Six now. He told me when we did a little blow before the race, so I paid Tracy to, you know…"

Oh, really? Is that what alias Six said? That little weasel. And, of course, I know what you pay Tracy to do for you.

"Don't be angry with him about the coke. It was my idea," he adds, and before I can explain anything, especially the fact that there is nothing between Six and me, the bus whips by us.

Four starts the engine, catches up to the bus, and delivers me underneath our hill at the same time. I get out of the car, and as I close the door behind me, I hear his voice through the window, saying, "Mia, I am really sorry."

Chapter Thirty-Five

Paige – The Leader

I predicted this was going to be a good day. I even got to the base early again this morning as if I knew my leader would be here. He has become my challenge, and my days are filled with memorizing our drills.

I enter the gym. He sees me right away and beckons me over, signaling me into a fight.

Really? A bit arrogant today, aren't we? Well, a fight with him is what I want, but I already don't favor the type of mask I was given today, so yes, I will probably get my ass kicked. Damn it.

After the training, I sat in the car and replayed the whole morning in my head multiple times. The unbelievable speed of the leader's moves and their perfection. It's torture watching how good he is. *A freaking master.*

When I stepped into the fight with him, he advised me first that there was no hold or choke aloud today, so we would go only for hits. Once one of us gets ten hits in, we move on to the archery level and the ball launcher before returning to the fights.

There was no surprise that he quickly got his ten hits on me. He stopped our fight several times to explain what I needed to work on while touching my arms and hips into the right stance. He hasn't touched me quite like that before, so it made me wonder if he is starting to like me better now.

After that, the archery and the ball launcher were my type of competition, so he didn't have to coach me through any part of that. He was working with other cadets at that point anyway, so he only saw my results afterward, but I knew he was stunned as I completely nailed it.

I knew I was known around the base for this. No item could be thrown at me that I couldn't catch perfectly or dodge. I only missed twice at the archery level by a few centimeters. My overall stats were great.

Then I met up with the leader again, but we didn't get to finish the whole fight set because I got scratched on the neck, and the cut was bleeding too much to keep going. So, I was called out.

Still, outside of that, the exchange tempo between me and the leader felt terrific. I could tell he was taking me seriously and was enjoying our rivalry.

We bowed to each other silently at the end, and he signaled me to take care of the wound on my neck.

He also pointed between us, changing it into a spiraling motion in the sense of "this to be continued," and I nodded. I can't wait.

Chapter Thirty-Six

Damien – The Hunt

Rob asked me if I wanted to come with him and watch his practice. I don't mind getting out of the heat, so why not. Plus, this may be a way for us to hang out.

I then watched his team play scenarios, shootouts, suicide drills, and all of that for an hour. I get now why Rob is ripped the way he is; hockey sure isn't easy.

After the practice was over, he drove us to a bar.

Once we walk inside, the bartender looks me up and down like she's unsure of me, but Rob says, "Don't worry, Paige, he's about a month legal."

I fleshed my pretty driving license at her while checking her out. This girl is something else.

She has medium-length, thick brown hair and beautiful green eyes. There are the kind of eyes that will captivate you by the depth behind them. I also checked out her body, and damn, she is fit. Plus, her beauty stands out with how sure she is of herself as if she wouldn't care what anyone thinks. Simply said, she is smoking hot, and her confidence makes me want her like crazy.

"Oh, trust me, we all have eyes on Paige," says Rob, who obviously saw me staring at her. I am glad we can drop my stupid attempts in their language and speak in English.

"She is…" I start while breathing out my excitement openly, but he jumps right back, adding, "Oh, yes, she is, but Four comes here to play poker once in a while, so you better hurry if you wanna have a shot at it."

And I would go and try, but at that point, Paige's shift was over, and she was packing up.

She waved goodbye, and my eyes followed her to the door before I could land back on Earth again and start paying attention to Rob. And we got into some real and heavy stuff.

He told me all about how their pops died and how Anna had been taking strong meds for her depression for years. She was almost to the point where she would want to end it before she met my Dad. That night of the crash changed them all, and mostly Mia.

She has been struggling to connect with people ever since. Even though she is very smart, she doesn't work the same way as the rest of us and probably never will.

Rob believes she is broken inside, and that is why he is in this overprotective mode around her, making sure she doesn't get hurt again. Hence, the scenario with Four.

Rob would take a bullet for the guy, but Mia comes first.

Apparently, Four takes drugs and girls to keep him going, and none ever says no to him. He is one scary animal and has no respect for life, making him a wild card and no match for Mia whatsoever. They are nowhere near the same level or compatible.

We then wrapped it up at the bar. The rest of the day should have been easy, but since we got back to the Trap, I had the feeling that something was cooking up. Rob and Four exchanged looks a few times, and when pops wasn't paying attention, Four pointed at the ground, but I didn't see anything there.

I knew they wanted me to leave for the night, but I said I was going to stay. Once Dad's car lights were far in the distance, Four went to the truck and pulled out his gun.

Rob says, "Let's get some sleep," but my question goes to both of them, "Where are you guys going?"

This time, Rob answered me in English. He says, "Something is taking the animals from the barn; we have to get rid of it. We start hunting at the first light."

I can't help but point out, "But Dad…"

"Yes, Dad would call a cavalry, I know, but we don't need that. Four will shoot the living shit out of it, trust me. Let's have some fun. But you can stay at the house unless you want to come with us. Are you staying?"

"Hell no," I say, feeling powerful.

We then crashed at the lake house, and both of them were

sound asleep all night, but I didn't close my eyes for a second. It's still dark outside when I see Four already moving around the house and grabbing his gun. Once Rob is up, we quickly get ready to go. Rob also grabs a gun, and we are walking into the woods.

Rob is next to me, and we are trying to catch up with Four at the front, but he is on a mission this morning for sure. Rob whispers, "It could be a wolf or maybe a bear. Every time it comes, it destroys the paw prints by dragging the calf away with it, so we can't tell by the tracks. No matter what you do, though, stay behind Four. Don't go and do something stupid."

Oh, trust me. I am not getting any ideas like that.

"Okay," I whisper, and he slaps my back. "No worries, Four will take care of it. His Grandpa taught him how to hunt." *Yes, and I bet it was in foster care. It must have been one hell of. I call bullshit on that.*

At that time, we were walking down a steep hill and must have been approaching the barn because I could smell the cows and the horses, all of it. I even heard the chickens fussing.

"I'll try to get it in the gut but fuck, I don't even know what this thing is," states Four, and that doesn't give me much confidence. I think I am going to shit myself before we get to kill anything.

He then adds, "We should start chasing the animal a bit. I

need a good stance to shoot it. You got my back, right?"

"You bet, I got your six," comes from Rob, but to me, it all sounds only like many dangerous words in a row.

Then Four starts howling, and that is actually it for me. I am freaking done playing Indiana Jones.

Thankfully, the sun is almost up, but then, all of a sudden, Rob pushes me, and I fall into the mud on the ground behind him. They both started shooting, and before I knew it, they killed what looked like two jackals. I have never seen this animal in my life, but it is a smaller version of a coyote with a stronger bite force.

We then soon after found an injured calf, which was ripped up pretty badly, so they had to kill it as well, and yes, I kept throwing up throughout the whole damn thing.

I blamed it on Four because he was the one who ripped out the guts and any inedible parts out of the calf. Then he left it there in the forest for scavengers to feast on, and by that, my stomach was turning without stopping.

Chapter Thirty-Seven

Mia - Let's Go

I can't believe it. I sit in this beautiful, freshly stolen car, and my hands won't stop shaking. My head is on a repeat of Four's words. *Just stay at the back and watch your mirrors.*

Then I heard Izzy's voice through my opened window. "You look like you need a good luck kiss."

She moves closer, and while looking into my eyes, she licks the white powder line from the top of her hand. *Yes, no, yes, no, yes, no.... yes.* I nod, and she leans in for the kiss. I love her lips.

She then moves back a bit, so I grab the bottle of water on the seat next to me and chug down almost half of it together with whatever powder she just left dissolving in my mouth. She leans back in and licks the remaining water off my lips.

Okay, she is getting me pumped up more than I thought I could get. Damn, I don't want to stay at the back anymore. I want to race now. I want to win.

She sniffs in whatever she had left on her hand and then says, "God damn, you are it for me, Trinity."

I smile at her once more, but at the exact moment, I spot Four's eyes watching through the side mirror of his car standing in front of me.

His energy is on the high, and I read his lips, saying, "What the fuck?"

Too late. It is here again. The weird high and hyper mash-up of feelings. I can do anything. I want more of it. I suddenly feel so confident and want to have all types of meaningless conversations with anyone. It freaks me out. And what I want most is the guy that I am looking at. I can have sex with him right now if I walk over there, and I think I love him. Let's go, let's do this.

And the gun goes almost in the exact second.

I immediately step on the gas because I am definitely not staying at the back, not with the pump I feel right now. We are speeding down the road; I feel the car's energy and would be in the lead if Four wasn't blocking my way.

Damn, how am I gonna get around him?

My eyes flicker between my mirrors, and now, I see it. Alias Three. Con. He comes from the left and looks like he is going to hit my side head-on. *Con, you are too obvious; you can forget about it.*

I hit the gas harder, making my front bumper tap Four's car a bit, but at least Con ended up crashing into Five behind me.

Then, the road in front of us forks into two directions.

Four goes left, so I go right.

I am literally flying down this tiny little road, but it is like I can see for a mile ahead. Then, a corner of my eye spots red and blue lights flashing somewhere on the left side of the forest.

Damn, that's the cops. Four is heading straight towards them, but I need to take care of myself right now.

My body is pumping like crazy, and I am not even sure I am going the right way, but I keep pushing the gas pedal lower and lower.

There. I see it. The name of the village. Okay, I am still on the right track, but at the same time, I feel I have someone on my tail. That sneaky one has the lights off and is just following me, but the driver's energy is too high not to notice.

Sure, why not. I can play the game. I can do anything right now.

I turn my lights off then as well and keep on driving.

Without using the brakes, there are no lights to give me away, so we are both riding blind. It's slowing me down, but whatever.

Bang. The car behind me just hit a tree. I hope someone will come to help whoever that is, but I can still feel the driver's energy. He is pissed but unharmed.

Now, it's almost too easy for me. I could even win this thing. I see the city lights in the distance. I am turning onto the main road but don't see Four anywhere. I hope the cops don't have him, but he is probably already smiling at the finish line.

If I get in second, I'll be happy.

Dang it, my speedometer was at 170 kilometers per hour, and I just flew over some train tracks. Then, there was a weird sound coming from the car. There were some sparks, but they died immediately. Still, the car suddenly smelled like fire.

I gotta keep moving. There, I see them now. Chris, Izzy, the finish line. Oh my, is this for real? Oh God, I am first. I won! Where is Four? I hope he is okay. Is he gonna do time if the cops got him back there?

I stop the car and hear some voices yelling from the outside, but I am too deep in my thoughts. I can't focus on anything right now. There is a sudden light behind me; another car must be coming in, and the thud on my window gets even louder, but it doesn't matter. I need a moment. More banging on the glass. I need to think. Now, it's like someone trying to break into the car. Just let me be. The sound is annoying. I finally snap out of it and look that way.

Four is standing on my left, trying to smash the window with a rock, and his energy is almost desperate. He keeps yelling, "Get out of the freaking car! Now!"

I grab my water bottle and swing the door open. Some hands grab and pull me out, someone throws a blanket over me, and we are running.

I am now being pushed into a van, and we are moving. I take the blanket off of me.

"Hey, crazy lady, what happened to you staying at the back like I told you?" says Four who is sitting next to me on the floor in the back of a van. There are six people with us.

Everyone is cheering, laughing, and whistling as well.

I lean into Four's shoulder, and he kisses my head.

He hands me his water bottle with some juice left in it. I take it from him and swing it back, finishing it all.

Chapter Thirty-Eight
Mia – The After-Party

Twenty minutes later, we got out of the van at what can only be described as a mansion. A beautiful glass house on the top of a hill, hosting a huge party.

Chris, who was driving, got out of the van and turned to me, smiling and saying, "Trinity, my queen, this is for you. You can have anything. Just name it."

I am already freaking out. The overload of different energies, all the voices, and the various smells around us.

I hear, "Yo, yo, yo" from the crowd, and it's like a moving train. On top of it, everyone seems to have the urgency to look at me, talk to me, smile at me, and touch me. *Please don't.*

I grab Four's hand desperately, and he asks, "Are you okay?"

No, I am falling to pieces over here. Am I saying this out loud? I feel like he's not hearing me. I am not going to make it. Please help.

He wraps his arm around me while using his other hand to push away people who are trying to grab at me. We now see a guy coming our way, walking fast towards me, and it's hard to say what his intentions are, but it looks like he is angry. Four gets him to the ground with a single move. I always knew Four was strong, but wow, that was pretty impressive.

We stayed at the party for about three hours after that, and Four didn't leave my side.

I had a few drinks but kept wrapped in his strong arms, not moving much. I am coming down from the high, and I feel the lack of energy is getting to me already.

At some point, Four leans in, and I feel his temple on the side of my head when he whispers. "Do you want to leave? Should we head out?" I nod. *I am ready to go.*

We then get on his bike, and I wrap my hands around him tight. My head is pounding, so I try to relax and let Four take control. We ride down the road about twenty kilometers when I feel this weird rush of tension before us. I tap on Four's shoulder and show him to slow down. He does.

Within another few hundred meters, we are being pulled over by a cop waiting on one of the side roads. Four turns his head back to me and asks, "Do you have drugs on you? Should I make a run for it?"

I don't say anything, but I realize the little bag Izzy left with me still sits nicely in my pocket. If I tell him, he will go for it and either get us killed or arrested. *No, it's okay. I am feeling the cop. He is not here for me. All of that energy goes towards Four.*

At that point, Four pulls over, and we're stopped. The cop asks for Four's license and papers, then presses the radio to his mouth, "Hi Helen, can you run a 10-29 for me?"

After that, he started reading our plate and the numbers out of Four's license before stating the words out loud. "Quain Thomas Zeller."

I turn to Four, surprised, and he confirms, "Yes, I am Quain. That's my actual name."

At that exact moment, Chris sent a message to the group chat: "Alert. Four has blue on him. It's the following 10-20." And the next message gave our location.

The cop then comes over again, lets Four blow into a breathalyzer, and makes him walk in a straight line.

Four is clean tonight. If the cop had asked me instead of all this, we would have saved all of us some time.

He returns the license to Four and says, "Okay, love birds. Have a safe drive home."

Four gets back onto his bike, and before he puts his helmet back on, he asks, "Am I dropping you off at home? What's your curfew?"

I shake my head and confess, "I am actually "working" tonight, so we're good. I faked a shift."

"Okay," he says more cheerfully. "What do you wanna do then?"

I smile and ask, "You don't know?"

He stops rustling with the keys, grabs his helmet underneath his chin, and takes it off.

Look at that spike in his energy now. Oh, yes, Four. You are getting laid tonight.

"For real?" he asks, and I can count the beats of his heart, how loud, strong, and quick they are coming through right now. I put the helmet back on my head and said, "Yes, for real."

Chapter Thirty-Nine
Paige – A Boat Party

I am heading to a boat party where I am to work tonight. It came as a favor to Steve, the bar owner, my boss. He is a nice guy who trusts me with more things than a shift on a boat, so why not. The party is enormous, and I can see it from pretty far away.

Once I got over to the boat, I was asked to run the bar on the main deck and get two girls to help with stuff because the boat was packed full. So crowded that people were literally stepping on each other's toes from bow to stern.

We are getting the drinks out, and I feel good. I don't have to be on watch like in Steve's bar, so I can relax a bit, and time goes by fast. Steve also showed up at the boat and walked up to me at the bar around midnight. He started with his typical, "How's the night going?" before slapping a coaster on the bar and sliding it towards me. Then he said, "That's this month's batch."

I pulled the coaster my way and then hit it in my pocket. I know there is a USB stick underneath that only Steve and I can get into. We both have the twenty-four-digit password containing letters, numbers, and special characters. I don't know where he's keeping his, but I have mine tattooed into my memory. I don't keep a physical copy of it anywhere. I have been hacking and uploading data onto this stick through my proxy for about six months now.

I offered Steve a drink, but he didn't want to stay long, which made me confident that the stuff I am hacking and loading onto the USB stick for him was really dangerous. *What is he getting me into?*

I shook that off once he left and listened to the music for a while before I saw more people coming to sit at the bar.

This particular group was five guys who were so deep in their discussion about tonight's race that I had to ask them about three times what drinks they wanted to order. I hadn't finished with them yet when one of the guys followed the sound of an incoming car coming from the road near the marina and yelled, "Guys, there he goes."

The noise made me look in that direction, and I saw a black car literally flying by. The crazy speed made me pause while others turned their heads, some gasping as they looked. I noticed a few voices saying, "Woah," and one of the girls ran to the side of the boat, yelling, "Four, I love you!"

"Isn't that the girl you were after?" asked a guy sitting at the bar, and his friend frowned before answering, "I guess she is into Four, but it's too late to follow him tonight anyway. He's far gone."

It made me smile and somehow happy, knowing I was not part of that game. Trying to find someone. That life was never meant for me, but I am okay with it. I am okay alone.

The rest of the night went smoothly. I was even bored and ended up people-watching and listening to music again, and then I was on my way to my car.

It was a long walk as I parked all the way up on the road in the middle of the west side neighborhood. There was just no way to find any closer parking than that. The marina parking lots were too packed earlier to find a spot.

It got me scared at first, thinking that my car got nicked as I saw police lights on the road in front of me. Then, the closer I got, the surer I was the target tonight was not my car but somebody else.

I see a guy standing ahead, who must be the owner of the missing vehicle, and who is now literally jumping around the police officer standing along the bushes where the car was probably parked before it got stolen. He is yelling, throwing swear words around about the damned racers, asking the officer how long it will take them to do something about this.

"Can I help you, mam?" asks the other officer standing in my way.

"My car is parked over there," I say, pointing to the side of the road behind him, where my little red beauty sits, waiting for me.

"Well, you are lucky," came from the angry theft victim and was directed to me.

"Where are you coming from?" the officer asked, and I told him about my shift at the boat. He was curious if I hadn't seen anyone driving a black Toyota Supra tonight, and I answered with the only part of the truth that I could. "I don't really know what that car looks like, officer, so I am not sure, sorry."

With that, he let me go.

Chapter Forty

Mia – The Search Within

Last night with Four was super weird.

"You scare the hell out of me sometimes," he said while looking through his phone, as apparently, after the race and my win, I was the talk of the chat.

He then added, "In the car, at the finish, you were like zoned out or something, I was shitting myself. And the other things? Nobody rides without the lights on, and the way you knew about the cop waiting, care to explain all of that?"

"I see and feel things. The energy of things around me and the energy of people on different levels," I said slowly, expecting the shock and disbelief I normally get from people, but he just nodded. "Yeah, I thought it was something like that, but you are not racing again, all right?" He then closed his eyes. "The whole thing was brutal. If Rob would know about any of this, fuck I would be dead."

Why is he going about Rob right now, and what the heck is wrong with his energy?

I noticed a change within him tonight.

Perhaps he was expecting another crazy episode when having sex. Still, I was coked up the last time we did it, and I am usually not passionate like that. It took me years of therapy sessions to be able to express my feelings, and even with that, I am still not the best at it.

On top of all, the coke aftermath was not my thing, so I am not planning on doing that again any time soon. With that comes the fear of Four's size, which I felt tonight fully as I was sober. It's just too much for me to handle.

And somewhere there, I also feel he needs more to keep him going than only my soft touches and cuddles.

Chapter Forty-One

Damien – A Fish

"What's that?" Four asked.

I look through the plastic bag I hold to check on the little goldfish idiot inside and then say, "There was an accident, and one of Mia's fish died, so I bought her a new one."

Rob cringes his jaw a bit and utters, "Uh oh."

"No worries. I picked the exact looking one at the store; she'll never know," I stated calmly and started walking up the stairs when I heard that chuckle behind me. So I turned back and asked, "What's so funny?"

Four shakes his head. "Nothing. It's a nice try, but she'll know."

"How would she? The fish have names or something?"

He grinned slightly before saying, "It's not the fish; it's you."

Whatever, dude. I know about her mind-reading thing.

I pull my chin forward and say, "She will not know if I don't think about it around her."

Four still looks at me like I am not getting it. He keeps rolling the lighter in his hand before adding, "It's not about that, dude. She feels the energy. A lie, someone's guilt, whatever it is."

Rob closes the fridge he was rummaging through and turns around with a question, "And how do you know about this?"

Four stops the lighter from the next turn and says firmly, "Because I know a thing or two about her now."

"Yeah, I'll tell you what," Rob jumps up to sit on the counter, "I think you better shut up about you and her."

"Why?" asks Four, turning in his chair around to face him. Rob stops gulping and pushes himself off the counter, throwing the empty shake bottle into the bin in the kitchen.

Then he leans a bit forward, and it's like he's speaking to someone with no comprehension when he asks Four, "Why? Do you really wanna go there?"

Now Rob's hands are free, and he is clearly getting pissed off. I can tell even before his following words start to gain more temper. "After all we've done. After all, that I've seen?"

And I know what he means. When Four was tipsy, he mentioned parties where they did a girl or two together.

"That was before her, and you know that," Four argues quickly, but I don't think he's using the right tone for this, as Rob is already in his face. "Yeah? How much of it all does Mia know?"

Four stays quiet, so Rob triumphs with, "Exactly. And you

are not going after my sis, facts. Have your fun with one of the race skanks or at the bar, why don't you. Leave Mia alone."

And that gets Four's interest as he asks, "Yeah, about that, how much do you know about the bartender at Steve's?"

Rob smiles and briefly looks at me before saying, "Paige? I know that she's hot."

Four rolls his electric eyes. "Yeah, people keep saying that, but I am interested in her getting out of the Sweptail at the race."

Rob stops lifting a cookie to his mouth and asks, "You mean the Sweptail of the RF?"

Four nods and Rob thinks aloud, "She is not working guys, so she could be a recruit. She could be trained."

That makes Four nod again and state, "Oh, I am ninety-nine percent sure that she is."

With that, Rob is already on his feet and heading for the door, saying, "Well, let's find out for sure then."

Chapter Forty-Two

Paige – Truth or Dare

Tonight is not a hockey game night, so the girls don't have much to do and stay close to the bar area. They ordered a few drinks and now talk about everything, and I mean literally everything.

When I get bored by their sex stories, I move on to cleaning underneath the trays when suddenly Carly rushes over to me and asks, "How do I look? Is my makeup alright?"

I am about to respond to her, but she is already adding, "Rob is here."

That makes me look up, but it isn't Rob who I find standing in front of me now. It is Four.

His eyes met mine before he started with, "So, we meet again."

"What can I get you?" is the most uninterested question I could come up with. He answers coldly, "Martini, no shaken, no stirred."

I quickly make his drink and place it on the bar in front of him while trying to ignore his eyes. He grabs it, gives me a thank-you nod, and walks over to hang out with Rob, Carly, and Stef. *That is great because that way, they might all get out of here soon.*

It was around midnight when Carly's voice rang in the distance, stating, "Oh, Paige is awesome. She would kick your ass for sure!" *What the hell is she saying to them?*

It makes me look that way, but at that point, their whole bunch was already walking towards the bar, and Rob was the first to deliver. "Paige, I hear you play darts?"

"No. Not really," I responded quickly because I don't really do. I only played here once with the girls when we had a slow night. *I obviously shouldn't have.*

"So, you are not playing with us then?" he double checks, and I shake my head, so he starts walking away, adding, "That's okay. Chicks are never really that good anyways."

That statement pissed me off, so screw it. I say, "You know what, I'll play."

"But you said that we would only stop here for a second and then go see a movie together," reacts Carly in a disappointed tone, so Rob now shrugs his shoulders before turning back to me and adding, "Oh, sorry, I guess no darts for me, the movies are calling."

He then turns back to the group and says their way, "I guess Paige will be left only with the second-best thing over here." And then he places the darts into Four's hand.

"No, that's okay. We can play some other time," I say quickly, hoping they will all leave and take Four with them. *Please do.*

"I guess you're not so tough anymore, are ya?" Four's voice comes from behind my neck, and he kicks the back of my shoe, which makes me turn around and say, "Don't you dare."

His face lights up, and somehow, he brings even more arrogance into his voice when jumping in with, "Oh yes, that's a great idea. Why not? Let's bring truth or dare into the game."

I breathe out with a sigh, "Sure, why not."

"You kids have fun," Rob chuckles as he walks away.

Four is already walking over to the bar and getting a bottle of Tequila from Tom, the other bartender on tonight. Four then says, "Let's go with an easy Count-up. You call the number on the board you think you'll hit, and if you get it, you ask me a question. If I want to answer, I will do so, but if I don't, I say dare and take a shot of Tequila instead. And vice versa."

Whatever, dude. It's not like this is really about the game's rules now, is it?

Four throws first and calls out twenty as the dart is mid-air, flying towards the board. It hits twenty just as he says it would. I am sure we both know that I will not answer any of his questions when he starts asking. They will probably be only too personal. He will push me into a dare and try to get me drunk.

He asks, "Have we met before? Outside of this bar or the race?" *What a stupid question. I can answer this one.*

"Truth," I say. "No."

I see his eyes are on me like a freaking lie detector but whatever. I am telling the truth. He nods at me, encouraging me to throw. I move around him to get into position to take my turn, realizing his build again.

How does a racer stay fit like this? Every time he throws, I see his bicep flexing. It looks like it was carved into a moving stone. Damn.

We continue for a bit, taking turns throwing darts and taking shots. We clearly both don't want to answer any of the questions we ask.

"I am hitting twenty," I say, and I do. Then I ask, "Have you ever lived in a different country than this one?" *He better not lie to me. His accent is light, but I can hear it.*

"Dare," he says again, as he did almost to every one of my questions before and goes to the bar to pour himself a shot. I have been watching him closely. His physical confidence, his moves, and his control of his body language are more telling than he thinks they are.

I am sure that he's been trained. Perhaps trained at the same base as me? Is that possible? Maybe he is assigned by the RF to evaluate me, but he might be with the Pollwest. I once overheard

Tracy saying he was with the Marines or something, so who knows. Damn, he is irritating.

After that, I saw the last few people leaving the bar. Tom waved goodbye and left the bar keys for me to lock up.

Four is now walking back from there over to me, throwing darts on the way, hitting twenty on the board with each of them without looking. *What a show-off.* Then he asks, "Do you know how to fight?" *Oh, this is getting close.*

"Dare," I say, breaking away from his gaze and walking to the bar to pour myself another shot. It's my sixth, and the Tequila is undoubtedly getting to my head. Four returns there as well. He walks up beside me, and I am sure taking my time while putting the salt on my hand, letting him watch me.

"Wow," he shakes his head in disbelief and even chuckles. I throw away the slice of lime that I was just biting into after taking the Tequila shot. I turn to face Four's damn eyes straight on when I glare at him, "What do you want from me?"

"Nothing," he says, moving his face closer and then adding in a low tone, "But you should know that I see you. Since the pathetic keys drop at the race, I see you. Plus, saying to Tracy to have fun with the crackhead? Really? You better watch yourself, alright?"

I smile arrogantly and put a sweet tone into the following words. "I have no idea what you mean."

He walks away from the bar while imitating my tone and repeating, "I have no idea what you mean."

He then whips around.

"This," he says while throwing one of the shot glasses at me. When he sees it in my hand, he finishes accusingly with, "Is what I mean."

How did I catch it? Fuck. It was an instinct.

Now he's walking back over to me, and his gaze is fuming. My back hits the bar as he pushes me into it, and his lips start moving right in front of my eyes. "So now, listen to me carefully, Boot. Don't ever cross me."

*A Boot? Like a newbie? **Barely out of training?** Who does he think he is? Prick.*

My rebellious side is now moving closer to him and saying as firmly as possible, "Well there, cowboy, you better watch your back."

Four stays still for a moment, looking straight into my eyes, but it seems something moved within him, and he starts leaning in. *Is he going for a strike? Here? Now? Okay. Stay calm. Let it come. He is fit, and it will be a nasty fight, but your hands are fast, so you could make it. Strike below the chin.*

His breath is as close to my ear now that I can feel it all the way to my neck, which creates a weird shudder and anticipation of the fight, but then he starts slowly leaning away. Just like the freaking vampire would when backing off from the used prey.

He then grabs his keys from the bar and smirks at me arrogantly when saying, "Likewise. Nighty night, Boot."

Then I see the door close behind him, my body slides down along the bar, and my ass hit the floor with a thump.

He knows that I've been trained. What am I going to do?

Chapter Forty-Three

Damien – A Call

I am working with Four again. At this point, it feels like he is babysitting me. His hands are fully focused on work, but he shakes his head now and then, smiling in disbelief at whatever he's thinking about. He noticed me watching him and offered me one of his headphones. I grabbed it from him but now I am forced to listen to his style of music, but better than nothing. I guess.

Later on in the day, sometime in the afternoon, we are chilling and smoking what Four rolled up, which I think is the highest THC I have ever tasted. After another hit from the joint, he points toward my bicep and says, "Finally, you are getting some muscles there."

I was about to answer him with something cool, but his phone started ringing through the headphones we are both wearing. I don't bother taking it out of my ear, and he doesn't ask for it.

The coded voice on the line surely surprised me when it said, "Identify."

Four blows out his smoke calmly and speaks away from me. "SDA4A, authorize."

It takes about three seconds before the robotic voice starts speaking again, saying, "The profile you have requested is a seven-year training cadet currently awaiting an assignment. Completed T Maze with A awards."

Four utters to the side, "Arrogant bitch. I hope she'll fucking choke on it," then the voice continues on, "Three years in the air and two years in the field. Strengths: Krav-Maga, Jiu-Jitsu, shotgun, and a high control of thrown objects."

Four chuckled at that, then said to himself again, "Yep. The catch got her cover blown. She basically outed herself right in front of me."

Then he stands up to say, "Roger and out," and the line goes quiet.

He then offers me another hit and says, "Well, I knew she was not a newbie, but she's not assigned yet either. That is good because of the speed of her hands, damn; it's better to keep an eye on that, right?"

I smile again, like I do with everybody around here, but I am not as stupid as he thinks I am.

It is clear now why I understand him more than anyone around here.

He has an English accent in his words. Plus, he is here on a Special Duty Assignment, SDA, and that is how he identified himself to the computer voice on the phone.

Oh, I didn't say my mom's boyfriend is in the army, did I?

Well, nobody asked me.

Gotcha, buddy.

Chapter Forty-Four

Paige – A Night Glide

"Someone ran a search on you through the database, but apparently it wasn't Don," says Ronnie, once we sit in his car at the back alley again. This time, he is not picking me up for anything; we are only chatting.

I reply back, asking, "Who is Don?"

Ronnie takes a deep breath. "One of the elders. He looks you up from time to time. He likes you a lot."

He sees the disgusted look that showed up on my face and starts using his lecturing tone when adding, "Hey, it says in the files that you have not been intimate with anyone after the unfortunate rape incidents, so keep it that way, and if you pass the assignment, Don is willing to marry you."

Oh, goodies. Firstly, this must be the old creep that used to come to watch my training. How fortunate am I? Secondly, screw their files.

Ronnie continues in a more friendly voice when he advises, "Wake up, okay? This is the real world. If you don't pass your assignment, Don will buy you whenever he wants."

Well, I give him that. This is the real world, and I am not a princess. I am just another kid who was kicked out of foster care.

The RF owns me, but still, I would rather end myself before Don has a chance to touch me.

Ronnie now speaks his mind and says, "Who could be searching your file? Do you have any enemies within the RF?"

I shake my head, and he follows up, "Keep your eyes and ears open. They are getting your assignment ready. I was only told that you are going back to the race. Did you speak to anyone there?"

I am not telling you nothing, dude. I am a failure. I am not even assigned yet, and Four already knows I've been trained. Aargh.

I shake my head again; Ronnie puts his hand on my thigh and says, "You have been spotted running up the mountain in the mornings. Just keep training like that. You are a good girl, and Don is a decent guy. He'll be seventy next year, he will need someone trained and someone to care for him. He'd rather be married than alone, you know."

Yes, I know, and it might have just made me vomit into my mouth a bit.

I get out of the car, and the rest of my shift is a pure nightmare.

Everything is falling to pieces, and the anger is getting the better of me. I feel goosebumps on my arms, plus I am literally shaking. I need to get myself in control.

Thankfully, it's already pitch-black outside when I get to my apartment. I am too riled up and need to let loose. I grab my wingsuit and take it into my car. It's about a twenty-minute drive on the slow and winding road to the highest parking lot on the mountain. From there, I will still have to walk a kilometer to the place I am aiming for.

I finally get up to the lot and park the car. I will have to run up here in the morning to get it, but whatever.

I get dressed in my wingsuit and visualize the road before me. I have never done this so late in the evening; normally, it is still bright outside. I carry the weight of the suit for a kilometer to the rock, which is my starting point.

I take a deep breath, visualizing my steps. I must run thirty-five fast steps to the cliff's edge and jump off immediately. I check the compass on my wrist for the exact location, but why would that even matter now. *Let's get going.*

I start running. It is damn difficult, but I need this.

My legs are getting heavier and heavier under the weight of the wingsuit, and I feel my blood pumping all the way up to my ears. The wind is so strong today; I don't think I have ever been this tired, but I keep running. Thirty, thirty-one, getting close to the edge of the cliff and my breaking point.

What? Now. There. The silhouette of someone else. Who is this? No way! Another wingsuit? What are you doing? This is not funny, and this is not safe. This is only for me as I have a chute, and mainly, I don't care if I am dead or alive at the end of this.

Thirty-four, thirty-five, the last flat rock under my right foot, and I launch myself off the cliff's edge at the exact second. I spread my arms and soar into the air, looking back slightly to see the other jumper doing the same. We are both flying now. The full moon is out tonight, and I can catch a reflection of it in the lake below us.

What is happening now? Is this freak actually touching my hand? Why? Did he just pull my glove? You idiot!

I shake that off as fast as I can and focus back on counting. It's now about thirty seconds until landing. I can already see the other person's chute on the left side below me. We are getting closer. Now. I hit the black mirror of the water below me.

The water splashes up and is now in my nose, my throat, everywhere. I am coughing it out while trying to unzip the suit before it drags me down. *Come on, focus, and get rid of the chute as well.*

Now, I see a buoy floating nearby, but will I make it all the way over there? I start to swim for it, but the wind and waves from it are so strong, pushing me backward away from the buoy. I am running out of breath, and my muscles are getting weaker and weaker with every stroke. I realize this might be it.

I might actually die here today. And why not? It is not like I am going to let Don force me to marry him, fuck that, but if I don't do what the RF wants me to do, they will destroy me.

Finally, I reached the buoy and grabbed hold as tight as I possibly could. My lungs were literally gasping for air when I pulled myself around the side of the rocking buoy. I try to slow my breathing down while watching the other jumper pulling his chute out of the water on the shoreline. A man. Around two meters. Build. Athletic. Who is he?

Chapter Forty-Five

Damien – A Story

Well, what is happening here?

Anna is speaking to Rob in the kitchen, and he shakes his head in disagreement with everything she says.

She handed me a plate with bacon and eggs when I sat down at the table. I was hoping to understand some of the conversation as Rob seemed pumped for whatever reason.

"I didn't know what it was, but Mia started to eat better and even sleep better. It is since they are together. I think Four is good for her," Anna continues with a persuasive tone.

"No, he is not good for her," says Rob tiredly, but she doesn't seem to pay attention and continues, "Come on, Mia is in love with him."

Rob shakes his head and appears exhausted. Far from the version of him we normally see. He breathes out, clearly frustrated, saying, "There is no happy ending to this for her, and I will be the one to say I told you so when this all goes to shit."

"He is your best friend," Anna gently argues again, obviously hoping for more understanding. However, now Rob turns around the way I saw him do so a couple of times before. It means he's about done with being patient. "Mother, Mia doesn't really know him because not even I really know him. He is a wild card. True, he has been my friend for years, but there is a past to him that nobody knows."

Anna fights back. "That is not a nice thing to say. I mean, Four is acting out a bit, and I even heard a rumor about him using drugs, but the past before that was not his fault. God knows what happened to his parents, and he has been doing well when Zeller's took him in. It's a shame they moved so far away and left him here on his own."

At that point, Rob is grabbing his stuff and walking towards the door. He is obviously done talking about this. I drop whatever I am about to eat back on the plate because if I am not outside within thirty seconds, he will go without me.

"So, apparently, we have a happy couple in the house," he says sarcastically, even before my ass fully lands into the passenger seat of his car. I turn to him with the bottle he forgot in the kitchen, and with that, I spot his eyes. *Oh my, he really is pissed right now.*

I look at him as stupidly on purpose, as I am quite good at it at this point, so he explains, "Mother thinks that Mia and Four together is a good idea. I think it's not, but why would anyone listen to me, right?"

I plan to speak to him as gently as possible because he scares the living hell out of me, especially right now, so I ask, "Still, Mia can read him, right?"

Rob now sounds a bit calmer when speaking back, as if only thinking aloud when saying, "I guess. And I know Four doesn't mean bad. It's just who he is and the way he does things."

Then we get to the lake house, and I see Rob's eyes hunting for Four. He is somewhere at the beach, so I am sent over to get him.

I found him leaning on one of the giant rocks by the caves, and he welcomed me by passing over the joint he was currently smoking. *Sure! I'll take it.*

I sit down on the sand next to him, and he looks back at the lake house when asking, "Is Rob in there?"

I could answer, but I still like to play my game of not understanding, so I smile and say, "Nice."

He lifts his eyebrows and points his electric eyes at me when asking, "You still don't understand shit, or do you?"

I smile again, and so does he. Then he leans back onto the rock and continues without a single word in English, "Well, I'll tell you. Yesterday was insane. All the way to the edge, you know? And it's not like I am not used to weird things. I have been training the newbies for years, and they come with all kinds of skills, but this loony goes beyond anything. I mean, the jump she took last night. That was completely suicidal, but I know who she is now. There's no hiding that."

He takes another hit from the joint and then continues speaking, "I remember her from when I got to a new foster house forever ago. She was curled up on the floor there, beaten up to shit; those green eyes all swelled up. I helped her up, and her tears were all over me. She got transferred the next day to who knows where, but now, she is here. I still can't believe it's her, but do you know what she is like?"

With that, he looks at me again only to answer for himself. "She is like the thing you know will do you bad, but you're still gunning for it anyways; that's what she's like. I gave her a hint, though, if she gets in my way, I am gonna freaking kill her. What? You don't think I'd do it?"

I don't know why he keeps even looking at me. If he wanted me to understand any of it, he would have said it in English, so screw him. Plus, I just remembered why I came here in the first place.

I point back towards the lake house.

"Sure, let's go," he reacts, kicking the ground on the way up and saying, "The dirt is good today; I am gonna take the bike up to the mountain. Do you want to try it?"

A dirt bike? I don't think so.

I must have made a weird face as he added, "Don't worry, the ambulance will be here in a minute."

"Ha, ha," I say while literally walking by the ambulance. He parks it here every time before he goes for a night shift, as he will today.

Just about half an hour after Four leaves, Sabrina shows up at the Trap. She says that Knox and Drew are planning something new for tonight, and she asks me if I am in. I want to get laid, so of course, I say that I will meet her by the water in a few minutes.

Rob left for the ice rink a long time ago, and David wasn't asking me any questions when I was leaving the Trap, so I disappeared smoothly.

I met up with Sabrina as agreed and followed her to the car she had parked nearby. It is old and rusty, the engine sounds like a real piece of shit, but it's taking us somewhere.

When she finally pulls over, I see Knox and Drew waiting for us, holding a bunch of ropes, flashlights, headlamps, kneepads, and some gloves.

"What's that for?"

"We are going caving," Knox answers and looks at me surprised. Sabrina probably should have told me this, so I look at her the same way when repeating, "We are going caving."

"We might find some gems, dude. It'll be fun," says Knox, and I have had enough of being taken as a sissy girl around here, so

I say, "Sure, let's go."

"Maybe it's better if you leave your phone up here. I lost mine down there once before," says Knox while handing me one of the ropes. I tighten it around me, imitating his moves, and Knox adds, "I'll support you from up here, so you go down first."

"Okay," I agree, like the idiot I am. Still, Sabrina looks at me like I am a superhero, so I am pretty sure I am getting laid tonight for this.

They are dropping me down into the cave now, and I have already changed my mind about this whole thing. The walls of the black hole are cold, muddy, and slippery, and I am sure not seeing any gems in here.

I hear guys talking up above, but my body keeps dropping. The last voice that reached me was Sabrina's. "What is it? Is that a bear!"

Then everything goes quiet up there. *Are they freaking kidding me right now? Don't tell me they left. Fuck, Fuck, Fuck.*

"Guys, what's happening!?" I yelled, but there was no answer. I keep calling them, but of course, I get no response, and there it dawns on me that I fucked up. A few minutes go by, but it honestly could have been hours.

I am hanging on a rope, in a cold and deep shithole, only in my T-shirt and shorts, while my phone is up there. Well, if they didn't take it with them when they left, that is.

They better come back to get me!

Well, there is nothing I can do anyways. I am not a fighter. I never was.

Shit, don't say I was. You are still here. You are not dead yet.

Chapter Forty-Six

Paige – The Assignment

Another Tuesday comes with another poker night at the bar, but the night is really slow otherwise. I actually don't mind it. I cannot seem to stop that inner shake feeling that I've had since the jump last night.

I picked up my car in the morning from the parking spot up at the mountain and didn't see a soul in sight, but obviously, someone was after me last night.

Someone was searching through the database at the RF, and then someone threw himself off the cliff with me last night into complete darkness. It could even be the same person, or maybe not, but why would anyone do such a thing without trying to send me some sort of message?

Then, when I thought my day couldn't get any worse, I saw the door opening, and the elder, who was being introduced to me officially now as Don, walked in with two of his bodyguards.

Stef rushes over to the bar and whispers to Tracy, "Hey, he is an easy blow job, and the pay is always high."

That gets Tracy to lift her bum from the barstool, and she goes over to meet him. He wraps his arm around her right away, and they walk together towards the bar area. He requests a few drinks for himself and Tracy and starts an easy conversation. Still, I see his lustful eyes and am already not buying any of it.

As the night goes on and he is a few drinks deep, the alcohol clearly starts working its way to his head, and he is getting tired of the small talk. He turns to Tracy at one point and says, "Paige is stunning, isn't she?"

She nods, but he no longer pays attention to her and now directs his words to me. "I heard Ronnie told you about our deal. Perhaps you want to get a little taste of it tonight?"

Then he turned back to Tracy and said, "I think it's time that Paige takes one for the team, don't you?"

Seeing my cold expression, he pulls out a velvet jewelry box from his pocket. Inside is a beautiful diamond necklace. He turns it and points it at me. At the same time, I noticed Tracy's wide-open mouth stopped breathing for a second.

I slowly move closer to him, and his facial expression lifts slightly with clear excitement. I whisper, "You can pay and offer what you want, but you are never gonna own me."

While lifting his eyebrows, Don turns his face to the side and speaks to one of his bodyguards. "She is feisty this one."

Then he looks back at me and nods over both of his shoulders where the bodyguards are standing, pointing out, "Sugar, I can own you even tonight if I want to. I am a very powerful man. One way or another, you will be mine in the end."

Aargh! Gross!

Angry, desperate, furious. I feel all of those things, but I keep it in. I even give the creep a smile. I then hear people calling drink orders on the other side of the bar, so I move over there.

My hands are shaking like crazy, but I get the orders out as quickly as I can. When I go to place the last drink on a coaster, a hand slaps the bar surface right next to it. The palm starts lifting up when I look, revealing a glove underneath. My glove.

Only seconds have passed, but I am now looking into the face of the guy who wanted to make a statement by throwing himself off the cliff with me in the middle of the night.

It is Four. The freaking racer. Are you kidding me right now?

And that's it. All my emotions are meeting together, and I feel a colossal storm brewing deep inside.

I grab the glove, but I don't know why. I move around Tom, who is serving the next round and run for the exit door. I need a minute to breathe.

The cold air of the back alley hits my lungs at the same time that I feel someone grabbing my arm. I follow the touch with my eyes, and the glove flies out of my hand. Four is right behind me, looking at me as if he is about to say something. Instead, he grabs me by my arms, pulls me to him, and seals his lips on mine.

His tongue slides through; he tastes like a breath of mint; his body overwhelms me, and I freaking love it. I pull him closer to me, running my tongue around his, and it takes over a minute or two before my brain snaps me back to reality. *What are you doing?*

I shove him away from me. He is panting heavily while searching through my eyes. I am fighting with all the reasons in my head, screaming to myself this is not a good idea, but then the passion within me takes over. I throw myself back into him and slam his body to the wall behind him. He grabs hold of me again, sends his tongue back into my mouth, and his taste starts working its way through me like heroin.

His hands grab my arms hungrily now, and not only do I like it, but I demand more of it; I am pressing myself closer to him again, and we are both losing control.

The wind eventually blew into the alleyway and into one of the street signs behind me, and that sound made us both pull away. We stared at each other for a few seconds before my hand went up and pointed back towards the bar's back door.

I see his chest still breathing heavily in front of me when he moves his shoulders to have the T-shirt, which I messed up by running my hands underneath it, to fall back into the right place, and then he heads for the door.

I stay frozen in that alley, trying to stop my panic attack, when I spot a Sweptail pulling in. Ronnie then rolls the window down and asks me to get in the car. Once I do, he places a folder on my lap. It is my assignment. Finally.

Ronnie then briefly explains that my job will be to spy on someone and bring as much information as possible back to the RF. There is a chance of this person working as a double agent, carrying confidential data from our side but also from the Pollwest base. If that is the case, he is a direct threat to both, and if given the order, I will need to take him out.

Then Ronnie opens the file, and my brain stops working at that exact moment. My world is crashing down. I only feel the shiver running through my spine while looking into the blue eyes in that photo.

My assignment is Four.

Ronnie runs his fingers through the pages and relays, "His alias is Four. He appears to go by that name with everyone he knows. No records of his legal name in our files yet, as he is protected by the city, currently assigned as an ambulance driver. He is highly trained, and he has a lot of supporters in a lot of places, so don't trust anybody. He doesn't say no to drugs as he has access, so that should make it easier for you. Plus, he is also known to be a junkie for any girl that comes his way, so get him where you need him to be and work him over. We know he is a racer but not only part of the race. He is the race. He wins almost every time, so he's calling the shots. It makes him arrogant, and it makes him dangerous."

Of course, I wouldn't get it as easy as Anne, the last of the girl cadets assigned. She just seduced and pushed an old drug dealer down a flight of stairs. No, my assignment won't be like that.

Mine is a picture of a sex god who I don't seem to be able to shake and whose minty taste is still rolling over my tongue.

I leave Ronnie's car and walk back towards the bar. My head is spinning.

Four is now standing in the middle of the room, talking to the other poker players. My glove, which he must have picked up from the ground on the way back in, is visibly hanging from the back pocket of his pants.

I grab two beers from the bar, place them on a tray, and take them over to one of the tables on the floor. On my way back to the bar, when passing Four's back, I quickly reach for my glove hanging from his pocket, but his hand flies in and catches mine.

I look up at him, and now, our eyes lock together. A shiver travels through my spine as a reminder of what happened in the back alley just a few minutes ago.

Meanwhile, his other hand reached into his back pocket and slapped my glove onto the tray before me. His deep voice comes in with, "Jumping from that spot? In the dark? Boot, you are insane."

"So are you," I breathed the words out, freeing my hand from his, and walked away without turning back.

My shift was over before the poker night ended, saving me from meeting him again, at least tonight.

I get to my apartment, but I am sure there is no way I will be sleeping tonight. I put my running gear on, and I stormed out onto the street. I get into a fast pace right away, needing to get myself tired. I need to knock myself out entirely, and running is always the way to do it.

After I ran about two kilometers, I started to feel the sweat dripping down my skin, which was what I wanted, but at the same time, I hated it. I continue to run until I reach the lake just under the caves. The water looks lovely, so quiet and peaceful. I must wash the sweat off my body before it drives me nuts.

I took my shoes off and my T-shirt as well.

I guess it was not the best idea when I decided to wear the new red sexy lace bra and thongs today that Carly persuaded me to buy. I should have calmed myself enough at my place to change into a sports bra, at least before I charged out, but what's done is done. Well, I am keeping my workout shorts on; nobody is around here anyway, so whatever.

I then climbed up onto the rocks and jumped into the lake.

The cold water hits my pumping body straight on. It's like being thrown into a freezer. I quickly swim back up. My lungs are burning, and I feel the misty cloud my breath is immediately turned into, but I keep swimming.

I swam along the caves for about ten minutes, I slowly adjusted to the cold, but then I heard someone calling, "Knox, come on. Pull me up." *Am I crazy, or is it coming from one of the caves?*

I hear the voice again faintly, but it's definitely there, and it makes me curious. It may only be a prank, but there could also actually be someone in trouble. I look around a bit, and it seems like the only access to the caves is from the forest area above. I need to check it out, so I get out of the water and start running in that direction.

I am barefoot, and my breasts are barely covered in that pitiful amount of lace, but there is no other option. I must run up there quickly if someone needs help.

I am barely halfway up when I hear it again. "Help, please. Knox, this isn't funny. Drew? Is anyone there?"

Knox? Drew? I know both of them from the base. Are they in trouble, or is it somebody else?

I pull my strength together and run all the way to the top, but I don't find anyone when I get there. Only a rope is hanging down to the cave.

"Hey, who's down there?" I yelled stupidly, but it was the first thing that came to mind.

"It's Damien. I am stuck here. Do you see anyone up there? The guy Knox, is he there? Or at least do you see my stuff?"

I look around. "Well, there is a baseball cap on the ground," I yell back.

"Is there a phone in it?"

I grab it and say, "Yes."

"My code is 1414, and then can you please dial two? I have my friend on the speed dial."

And I did just that. It rang only once.

"Hey, little buddy. What's up?" says the voice I recognize better than my own.

Damien's friend is Four. Shit.

I breathe out loudly out of frustration and then say, "Hi, it's Paige. Damien is in trouble. He is hanging on the rope down a cave by the Devil's steps, and I can't pull him out by myself; plus, the rope is fraying over the edge. Can you send someone to help me get him out? And I mean, as fast as possible!"

"I'll be there in five. Do what you can. Do NOT let him drop. Please," he adds more gently than I have ever heard him speaking to me before. Then he hangs up.

I look around, feeling hopeless. Meanwhile, Damien keeps calling for help, pointing out that he doesn't want to die, bringing extra pressure to the urgency.

I ask him if he can try to stop the rope from swinging around so much, but he says he can't. I am watching the rope continue to fray, and I am freaking out. *I can't let him drop. What can I do? I need to put something between the rock's edge and the rope, what can I use? Think!*

I pull off my shorts and start crawling to where the rope hits the sharp edge. I could put them underneath somehow, but the ground is freezing, and the surface is slippery as hell. The edge looks more frightening than I thought it would. *Shit.*

"Are you hurt? Are you cold? What are you wearing?" I am yelling at Damien as I am getting closer to the hole.

"Not much. I am fucking freezing," comes back from him, and it is what I was afraid of. It must be getting hostile down there.

I reached the edge, but my body kept sliding closer, and this whole thing was getting out of hand. I am shaking, but I move even closer while fighting the rope until it dances onto the top of my shorts. That should dull the cut at least a bit, but this whole thing is getting worse by a second, as Damien is hanging only by a couple of threads now.

I lean closer to the hole again and yell, "Four should be here any minute," but at the exact moment, Four's crawling body shows up right next to mine. He lifts himself on his elbows, checks me out quickly, and snaps, "You are too close; pull back. Also, why are you naked? What the fuck were you two doing here?"

"I was swimming in the lake," I growled back at him. He turns his gaze to the hole and briefly speaks to Damien before moving back to safety. He ties two ropes around some big rocks and trees behind us, secures them with claps, and then throws the other ends down to Damien.

He explains how to tie them, and with that, Four comes back over to me. Without looking at me, he hands me a pair of gloves and commands, "Boot, put these on to help with grip."

Can he not even look at me? Calling me a Boot again? What a jerk. Sigh. What a freaking handsome jerk. His tall and athletic body is just asking to be touched. Shit. Put yourself together, girl. Stop looking at him like that!

With that thought running through my head, he is already kneeling down in front of me and tying a rope around my body. It lands on my waist just above the string of my red thong, which makes my blood rush up to my face, heating my cheeks with embarrassment before I realize things are getting even worse.

A cold breeze is now rolling in, blowing right between my legs, making me even shakier than I was when lying on the freezing ground before, and I know Four can feel it. Undoubtedly, he can see even more than he feels through the basically see-through lace covering a very small section of my body. *Why did I choose to wear this today? I am such an idiot!*

On top of it all, his fingers grazed my skin when he was adjusting the rope around me like a belly chain. His eyes paused when he noticed my tattoo running along the piercing in my belly button. *Damn it.*

My piercing and tattoo were a secrets for years now, as neither were allowed at the training camp, and I most definitely don't want some random racer to know about them.

At that point, he was already bending down to my ankles to tie the rope to one, which placed his head literally in front of my crotch. *Somebody, kill me, please!*

Thankfully, he was done by then. He stood up and started to tie the rope around his own body for a change. Then, after pulling on both of our ropes a few times, making sure they held strong, he walked closer to the cliff and dropped to the ground without saying anything to me.

I then walk over and lie down next to him, hoping that he can see how pissed I am. We start slowly crawling back close to the edge. The surface is freezing and somehow even more slippery than before.

"I am sorry," comes from Four suddenly and takes me by surprise before he adds, "But, you should have told me you need clothes. I could have brought you something to wear. You are going to be scratched to shit in that sex string that you are wearing."

I watched him saying those words, doing anything but making eye contact with me, still unable to look at me. What a shitty apology if that's what he was going for, but better than nothing, I guess.

When we get closer to the cave's edge, he lays on his back with his head pointing to the hole and crawls partially underneath the ropes, letting them run over his shoulder. He then looks at me, pressing his lips together for a moment as he considers something before saying, "I guess you have to get on top of me for this to work."

I run my eyes around quickly, panicking and thinking of other ways to do this. The ropes are too close together, and for both of us to be able to pull and not be in each other's way, I don't see other options either. *Damn it.*

After all, he is the muscle here; I can only support him. The skin on the bottom of my wrists and my knees is already cut up from crawling around in my underwear. I am tired, and if I lay beside him, I would not be able to gather enough strength to help him.

I breathe out then and nod in surrender. We will have to do it his way. "Fine."

I straddle over him before dropping down to my knees and placing my center just below his six-pack. Now, I lean over him, grab one of the ropes above his head, and he gets the other one.

"I'll say one, go, and we are pulling on go, okay, Boot?" he says, and I nod while trying to ignore that he called me a Boot again, together with the sweet heat of his breath. It's a mix of mint and chocolate, just like his taste. I remember it well. It's almost addictive and makes me blush again.

"One, go, one, go," he starts pulling, and no, there shouldn't be anything sexual about any of this, but my stupid body is deciding otherwise.

Oh my god, I am a sick girl. After years of not being interested in anyone, now I see myself on the top of a freaking cave, attracted to the worse son of a bitch I've ever met.

I am trying to keep it together while leaning onto the warmth of his body but seeing the muscles flexing on him is like a slap in the face.

And the worst part of it all is me. I am keeping my inner thighs cramped around his hips as much as possible, but for me to get enough strength to pull, I need to ground myself. Every one of my pulls on the rope is forcing me down onto his shaft that my body can feel pushing through his pants, and it feels like getting even bigger. *Fuck.*

Now, I am officially angry with myself and start pulling faster. It only causes me to get more speed and power into our rhythm, but to hell with it. I need to get out of this situation, as the thoughts in my head are getting out of control.

Seriously. I am literally riding him with not much of a barrier between us. Shit. Shit, Shit.

I am pulling the rope now with all my strength, breathing heavily. I see that I am making him super uncomfortable, but there is no other way to be done with this. Thankfully, it takes only another two minutes, and Damien is out of the cave. He is a little hypothermic, but he will be okay.

"We can take it from here, thanks, Boot," says Four my way immediately when I get off him. He throws me back my shorts. They are covered in dirt, but I throw them on anyway, needing to cover up at least a little. *Arrogant bastard. Screw him.*

I could have returned the gloves nicely, but I am pissed, so I slam them on the ground next to him and start walking down the path back to the beach without another word. I must go find my shoes and shirt as now, I really do feel naked.

Shit. I was so angry and must have taken a wrong turn somewhere back up there. I probably should have turned to the right. *Okay, let's walk back a bit to figure out where I am.*

I only take a few steps around the bushes but catch some of Four and Damien's conversation.

"Sabrina heard animals and freaked out, so I guess that's why they left," says Damien in an attempt to explain what happened, but Four's deep voice responded with, "Don't even. They left you here to die, so I better not see you around them ever again."

Damien replies, scared, "Are you gonna tell Rob about this?"

"Of course not, but you have no idea what you put me through up here. Next to her. Fuck."

Well, he really doesn't like me. Good. That makes things easier.

Chapter Forty-Seven

Damien – A Hole

I started calling again from inside the hole I was hanging down at, and then I heard a girl's voice yelling, "Hey, who's down there?"

Oh my god. Fantastic.

"It's Damien. I am stuck here. Do you see anyone up there? The guy Knox? Or do you see my stuff?"

"Well, there is a baseball cap on the ground," she says, and I come back with hope in my voice, "Is there a phone in it?"

"Yes."

"My code is 1414, and then, can you please dial two? I have my friend on the speed dial."

After that, everything went quiet again, and I was panicking. I guess she left as well. *Fuck.*

I start calling again. "Please get me out of here. I don't wanna die. Are you still there? Hey girl, can you hear me?"

Her voice sounds through the hole again, asking, "Are you hurt? Are you cold? What are you wearing?" *Thank god. She didn't leave.*

"Not much. I am fucking freezing," I answer but feel somehow better.

"Four should be here any minute," she says back after a while.

"Hey, little buddy, how are you doing down there?" Four asks me suddenly from above, and I have never liked hearing his voice more than I do right now.

He throws me some extra ropes. I don't understand why he thinks I would need extras, but I tie them around me as he says. Then I feel the pull.

He is getting me out of the freaking hole. Phenomenal.

Weird that he didn't fly in with the chopper that I've seen him piloting a few times, but still, he is my hero. I am now grabbing the roots and rocks as much as possible on the way up to help him out. When I get over the sharp edge, it rips a hole in my T-shirt, and I understand now why he threw me down the extra ropes. *Shit. I was about to fly and die.*

I am getting the ropes off of me, pissed like never before, but then I see her. The bartender from Steve's Bar. Paige.

Wow. I don't understand how Four got her stripped down to her lingerie for him that fast, but only one look at her is enough to get my blood pumping again.

I wanted to thank her, but my jaw was shaking too much, my teeth were chattering against each other like crazy, and anyway, she seemed somehow angry for some reason. She throws her gloves onto the ground and then is on her way. *What the heck?*

Four got the heat going in his car right away once we reached the beach parking lot, and I didn't know how to start talking.

"How come you didn't take the helicopter?" comes from me without thinking it through.

"Paige said you are at Devil's steps. That's too narrow," he answers unemotionally. He seems to be in his head, and I don't know why I said the next thing out loud. It just slipped out. "Did you see Paige? A freaking goddess."

With that, Four turns to face me, and if his gaze could actually kill, I'd be in trouble. He's prolonging the question in disbelief, asking, "Did I see her? Is that really what you are asking? Trust me, I did."

Then he continued before I got another word in. "She was pissed beyond belief, and I'll probably feel some of it in the morning," he mumbles.

Where would he see her in the morning?

I am then about to tell him that she will actually work the night shift at the bar tomorrow if that's what he meant. He noticed me taking another breath and quickly lifted his finger and thumb in front of my face while parting them for about 5 centimeters, adding,

"I am this close to running after her right now, so don't say another word about her. Please."

As you wish. I won't say a thing but look at your fluent English.

And with the same accent that my grandpa has. Bro, now I know where your home is.

Chapter Forty-Eight

Paige – A Solution

I haven't slept all night. I couldn't wait any longer and decided to drive to the base while it was still dark outside.

The guard at the gate is surprised to see me this early, but he lets me through.

I am pumped and furious. If Four would get in my way right now, I would probably try to kill him even without orders. *Who does he think he is?*

Well, he is a strong rival, so there is no room for any more mistakes. No more freaking butterflies in the stomach. Let's get this son of a bitch. I hope my leader is here today. I hope he will help me to get physically ready. If I pass the assignment, I might speak to the elders and promise myself a life of service, just if I am not forced to marry.

But my leader is not here. I go straight to the heavy bag in the gym, put on my boxing gloves, and start throwing punches. I hear myself grunting with every hit, but it's still not enough to make me feel any better.

I actually feel more frustrated than before I got here, and my legs started to kick the bag a while ago without me even realizing it. I don't even know how much time has passed before the voice changer sounded from behind me and made my heart skip a beat. The voice said, "Shift your weight better when you go for the cross."

I don't turn around. My legs started shaking just from knowing that my leader was here, but he moved to the other cadets working out on the floor without giving me another thought. *Obviously.*

I spent another twenty minutes on my cross and straight punches, and when I finally felt that I had enough, I went to have a rest on the bench. I almost tripped over it as my mask was fogged up. I should have taken a shield less one today. I reached underneath it and smudged some sweat off with my fingers.

"Why boxing? What's wrong?" says my leader, whose legs I see now standing in front of me. I shared a smile that he couldn't see and asked, "Can I kill someone just for fun?"

He doesn't respond, and I feel stupid now. "I am sorry, I didn't mean that," I say quickly in an attempt to fix it. He then crouches down beside me, and his knee bumps mine softly. *Yes, I started shaking again. Pathetic.*

He says, "Your anger is playing you. You've got to work on that. Remember our last Kumite fight?"

I nod, and he breathes out a smile through his mask. "Well, that's how I got you. Your anger gives you away."

With that, he briefly touched my thigh before I heard him stand up and walk away. I am melting, and he is leaving. Without knowing anything. Without knowing that apart from the kiss that I shared with that asshole Four, which got me into a sleepless night, I had never felt more intimate with a man before this moment.

Right now. Right here. With him. With my leader.

Oh my god! Am I actually falling for him? I guess so because I can't get him out of my head. I don't even know what he looks like. This is crazy!

I am still lost in that thought when I hear his disguised voice calling again, "Let's get it over with." Then he adds, "Thirty-six and thirty-two to the ring."

Shit. Thirty-six is me. I need to fix my mask.

"My mask is dud, it keeps fogging up," I quickly yell, and I am already staggering blindly out of the room. Thirty-two is Knox. He is tall and strong. I have seen him fighting, and he is probably going to smoke me, but I should at least get a new mask for the fight and keep some dignity.

When I walk back with my shield less new mask and enter the room, I see all the other cadets surrounding the fighting rink.

What the heck? Is the leader letting them all watch? Oh, he wants to piss me off again. That'll do it.

I stretched my neck, took my shoes off, and dug down underneath the ropes to step into the rink. In that motion, I see Knox is already on the move and ready to fight. *Shit.*

I raise my shoulders high and get my guard up. Knox is starting with a hands-down stance, which gives him the advantage of moving his head around easily. He keeps feinting, but with his hands down, he is open, which is arrogant and not the best defense. *I guess he doesn't fear me, but he better have some moves up in his sleeves because I am ready. As the leader said. Let's get this over with.*

I step in to attack and start throwing multiple punches. Exactly how I was trained to do. I am trying to move Knox onto the ropes and then going back into my peek-a-boo stance right afterward.

I stand tight, covering with the full length of my arms and making it hard for him to break through. So far, he's barely touched me, but I haven't caused much damage either. I am getting restless.

"Thirty-six, you got this," I am hearing from my left and another cadet seconds that with, "She could take him. This bitch is fast." *I don't know if I should take that as a compliment or an insult.*

"Focus," I hear coming from my leader. I am probably red in the face now; but he can't see that anyway through the damn mask on my head that is getting itchy already.

Knox hits his gloves a few times while moving around, and then he lifts them up in a motion of a time-out. I nod and he goes to fix whatever was bothering him inside his glove.

Meanwhile, the leader calls me into the corner. I go over to him and lean into the ropes to hear what he is about to say. I feel the dominance of his presence, and I smell his cologne also. *Shit. I freaking love it.*

I take a deep breath of it and hope he doesn't notice. He says, "Elbows in front of your ribs, not on the side, and if you won't focus better, he will knock you out. Is that what you want?"

OMG. Don't you see that I am trying? Just take your great smelling cologne away from me, and maybe then, I will try to focus.

I turn away from him, but at that point, Knox is done fixing his glove, and he is ready to go. Without any heads up, he takes two or three fast steps and starts striking with multiple jabs. Like a machine. *Shit.*

I am dodging as many as possible, defending, but then he gets me on my shoulder in a sensitive spot. The pain is so strong that it wakes me up, and my anger gets kicked up a notch. Well, Knox is the guy who put Damien in danger and who put me in front of Four's eyes in lacy lingerie. He is the one who made Four see my tattoo, my piercing, and probably more than that.

Oh, Knox, you are in trouble now.

My legs start moving, then I pause before him for a moment, rotate my hips, and while twisting my shoulder, I hit him with a leaping left hook. I smile underneath my mask because that was an awesome hit and must have hurt a lot. Then, I go quickly into it again with a combination of punches.

Knox reacts to it and steps in with a hook, but I managed to throw an uppercut before his glove hit my face. I got him in his jaw, and the power of the impact scared me for a second that he used to hit me again. I feel so much blood in my mouth, but I know I will get him back. I feel strong, furious, and free right now.

I am charging again, hitting a few times and already see that he is in trouble. I go in with another jab, and he is on his knees now but then suddenly, a whistle blows. I guess, one of the leaders standing by the door is ending our encounter.

My time at the base was up anyway for today, so I headed out to my car and drove back to my place but not feeling much better than when I was leaving this morning. Apart from the fact that I was able to punch Knox in the face a few times, nothing else changed, and I am getting nervous.

I need to figure out how I am going to go about tracking Four for my assignment.

Ronnie gave me only a few minutes to go through his file, that didn't have much information in anyway, so it's obvious that I will have to get the data on Four myself.

The job is to get close to him, but that is the last thing I want to do, as obviously, for whatever stupid reason, I don't seem to be able to control myself around him.

He is not in my head as my leader is, but he is super attractive. I can't even believe that I am thinking this, but only the memory of his taste is getting me back there with him, and I can feel his hands running on me again. Damn. I am screwed.

So, obviously, I need to stay away from him physically, dah, but I need access to him. Carly mentioned that Rob is his best friend, so maybe I will start there.

The only thing Carly knows about Rob is how to make him cum, and I need a little bit more than that. I started searching, and I went deep. Digging out any little detail I could find about Rob online. His hockey history and personal life, and I also detailed the rules of the game that he loves so much. Throughout his bio, I found out that he has a sister, so I will have to look into that tomorrow.

They are playing in the city, which means he is coming to the bar afterward.

Before heading to work, I put some makeup on and put my

hair up. I barely ever get dressed up, but I decide to throw on a fancier top for tonight. Then I head over to the bar.

Now, it's around nine in the evening, and I am enjoying the night.

The game is on, Rob is playing great, he has already scored. As I don't give a damn about the money, I placed a high bet on him to score a hat trick. He will hardly do that, but I might get his attention. I am most definitely getting attention and nasty looks from Carly, but I don't give a shit about that right now.

I need Rob.

I am not going to sleep with him, but I am ready to give him a night that he won't forget.

There. Amazing. He scored another one. I am watching him on the ice, and meanwhile, a memory of him right next to me comes back as a little hit into my stomach. Interesting.

Now, let's get back to the girl who wanted to order a drink. *I saw her at the race. Yes. Trinity.*

And, of course, the guy who is holding her hand. Four.

Can't look at him right now. Keeping eyes only on the girl. Four is ripped, I give him that, but my leader would kick his ass any day for sure. I wonder if Four was trained at our base and if he ever met my leader. For fuck's sake, I hope they are not friends. No, I don't believe my leader would have anything in common with this coked-up racer. My leader is smart and powerful. He is the type of guy you can see going hunting in the woods or flying a helicopter. Four is just an arrogant bastard who gets on my nerves, but if he is, after all, pulling some double-race agent shit, I am going to end him.

Now I am learning that Four is dating Trinity, who is actually Rob's sister. It is interesting to see Four's character being attached to anyone, but not surprising when you look at her.

She is the type of beautiful you would find on the cover of a fashion magazine or something.

There was a lot of work put into how I look tonight, but I still feel absolutely invisible next to her tall figure, porcelain skin, and perfect face. It makes one sad and jealous knowing these girls always have it easy in the world. What could bother a girl like that? Nothing. I bet her life is picture-perfect.

At least after I get their drinks out, both of them leave the bar, walk to the pool tables, and things get even better when Rob scores his third goal of the game. I can't wait for him to get into the bar because now, it's all just a matter of time.

Within an hour or so, I see the hockey players coming in, and then Rob comes up to me. We start talking. He is funny, his hair is still wet from his after-game shower, and he is attractive as hell. His body is literally massive, his posture sovereign, his muscles still pumping with adrenaline, and I know we will have fun tonight.

His eyes are almost hypnotizing when he asks me, "What are you doing tonight?"

I look around the full bar, smile tiredly, and say, "Probably killing myself serving drinks."

"Okay, and after you are done with that?"

His smile is so beautiful. His dark eyes are not holding anything back; he is putting it all out there as it is, and I love it.

I look straight back into his gaze and try to sound flirty when I say, "I am going to call it a night, I guess."

"Do you need a company for that?" *A real straight shooter. Fantastic.*

"That would be nice," I say because it bloody would, and I feel that my body actually shivers at the thought of a night with him. *What is happening to me lately?*

Four's voice interrupts my daydreaming. "Can we come too?"

I can't believe he just said that. What is this? Also, look at his lips. No, better if you don't. Shit. Focus.

"Sure," I say, instantly regret saying it.

They waited for me until I closed down the bar, and then we

headed to my apartment. Once we got there, Four was not waiting for anything. He is on the hunt, clearly.

He starts looking through all of my fake family photographs on my walls, commenting how lovely it would be for us all to go and visit my parents, asking how old I was in the pictures and where they were taken. *Simply driving me absolutely nuts.*

Then he picks up one of my fake soccer trophies from sixth grade of a school that I never went to, and he hisses as the edge of it cuts his finger. *That's what you get for snooping, prick.*

"I'll grab you a Band-Aid," I offer and start walking to the bathroom. He follows me there, stops right next to me and his cologne runs over me like an avalanche.

Let's hope he can't sense what his presence does to me even without a single touch. Damn it. I am pathetic.

I open the cabinet and notice his eyes already scanning through everything. My perfume, makeup, mouthwash, toothpaste, tampons, birth control pills.

He bloody knows everything about me now!

Then he looks at me and I see his eyes and face both cold as ice when he says, "Listen, Boot. I don't know what you think you are playing here, but you better fucking drop it."

When I raise my eyebrows, he leans even closer to add, "I

am not an idiot. I don't want to see you around any one of my friends. You got it? Or do you want a war?"

His body was dominating me, and I wasn't really expecting my rebellious side to show up, but it did when I smacked the band-aid on his finger, lifted my chin up, and responded with, "You don't tell me what to do, cowboy."

"Then you asked for it," he uttered before we returned to the other guys. They found a pack of cards under my coffee table, but we all refused to play them with Four here. Go figure.

Trinity turned down the option of playing darts with Rob for the same reason, so we ended up smoking some weed and playing the game Sorry. All while getting through a bottle of whisky, which was the only booze I had in my place.

"What's your number?" asks Rob, my way somewhere in the middle of the game. I can see he is tipsy, as he probably wouldn't ask me otherwise, but I know that idea it's going to piss Four off, so I like it. I grab Rob's phone and type in my number.

"Hit me with it," says Four Rob's way right after, and then they both ring through my phone. I dig it out of my chest drawer in the corner of the room and explain to them meanwhile that I don't actually use the phone very often.

Four literally snatched it out of my hand the second I pulled it out of that drawer, and he saved their names into my contacts. Trinity, whom I heard both Rob and Four calling Mia, which must be her actual name, is reaching out to Four now, so he lands my phone into her palm. She seems astonished when asking, "Why don't you use it? Such a cute little thing."

Oh, wow, where should I start? With the fact that I have never actually tried to make friends before and outside of Carly, who forced herself into my contacts pretty much the same way Rob just did, I don't have anyone to call. The base has been my only friend and family for many years now. Plus, this little sexy thing in a plastic case is a freaking tracking device that I don't want on me ever.

"I like my privacy," I say truthfully as I feel Four's eyes on me still. He is watching me like a hawk.

"At least take some pictures with us," says Mia, and Four offers his phone for that. *Of course, he does. I would also take as many pictures as possible of his apartment if I would ever get into it.*

Chapter Forty-Nine

Mia – A Bar Night

Four and I are now officially dating.

Someone saw us leaving his uncle's boat the other morning, and the truth was out before we knew it. Mom demanded that I get birth control the second she heard Four's name mentioned, so I guess his reputation got to her as well. I actually know he doesn't sleep around as much as people say he does, but he likes to keep the racer image of an asshole for whatever reason, so he is not disputing anything. I know him well. I know about him and Tracy, who gets him off now and then. I also know about the girls Rob pays to do the same thing for him, but whatever. They still take me for a young girl, oblivious to the real world. Rob is still throwing fits about the idea of Four and me together, but there isn't much he can do about it now.

I am not working tonight, so Four asked me if I wanted to go bar hopping.

We leave the house right after dinner, but I am already scared of the noises and the overload that usually comes with this type of fun. Four is holding my hand, so things are looking good so far, but the truth is, I wasn't expecting to be watching a hockey game on our first official date.

Well, it is literally playing on every TV in the bar, so whatever, I can take it for one night.

As we get fully inside, I slow down and start reading the energies in the room one by one and there. What is that?

"Wow, look at her," I say because I literally stopped walking when I saw the aura of that girl. "So beautiful and a perfect match," I add, and Four replies. "Who do you mean?"

I nod towards the girl behind the bar watching the game, but above all, obviously watching Rob, and I point out, "She won't take her eyes off of him. Look, and it's funny because Rob was asking about her as well. Of course, he would; she is gorgeous."

I have never seen a girl's body this firm and toned while also beautifully feminine.

"Why the make-up?" he thinks out loud, but then he adds, "Her name is Paige. Do you read her?"

"Yes," I say, then adding, "And no. She is red, just like Rob and you, but so powerful that her energy comes in waves. It's like an overload."

"Yeah, that makes sense. She is a lot," comes from him judgementally, and just when he finished saying that, her energy disappeared again. And now, it is back. *Interesting. What else can I feel about her?*

"There is a lot of anger there, pain also, and passion. She is a badass bitch and absolutely amazing," I stated before realizing that I had just said it out loud, so I quickly closed up with, "They will be awesome together. I don't think Rob will need two girls for his nights anymore."

Four turns to me quickly and urges, "Please never tell him that you know about the girls."

"I won't," I say, but his energy at that moment makes me switch to reading him.

I guess I should not have said all of that about Paige, as it feels like he doesn't like the idea of sharing his best friend with this girl. So much of his anger energy is going towards her now. Damn.

With that, we reached the bar; Paige looked at me and asked, "Hi, what can I get for you?"

I am about to say it, but the bar goes blasting at the exact moment as Rob just scored his second goal of the game. The other bartender then runs over to Paige and hugs her.

"I am sorry," she apologizes when she turns back to us and adds with a happy tone, "I put a lot of money on that guy tonight."

"That's my brother," I yelled at her over the noise of others around me still celebrating, and I felt Four squeeze my hand.

"I am hoping for a hat trick from him," Paige adds joyfully, and I can't help but be hypnotizing her face. I stare into her green eyes. She is beautiful and captivating. Then she asks me, "Bellini?"

I nod but have no idea how she guessed while she also placed a drink in front of Four, but he doesn't even look at her. His energy is super high now, almost at a furious level.

What the hell? He needs to chill, but it's not like Paige likes him either. When I read her from now and then her vibration goes really low when she is looking at Four.

He grabbed his drink and started pulling me away from the bar. I looked back at Paige at least one more time. *I want to feel her energy again. It's as gravitating as a magnet.*

Four, though, really couldn't have walked any further from Paige than he had. All the way back to the pool tables. We then started talking and got into playing Eight-ball for a bit, but he still didn't seem to be getting in a better mood. At least his energy is calmer, but not for long, as the guy playing darts next to us suddenly yells, "Paige, look, Rob's got that hat trick! Baby, you are cashing in tonight!"

Everyone is looking back at Paige now, and I look over at her as well. Her happy energy has just pushed her vibe into simply electrifying, but then it disappeared again. *Torture.*

"Maybe she is in love with Rob," I judge out loud while still looking at Paige. Four hits a corner shot and snarls, "Nice try, Boot." *His anger just hit the highest spike ever there. What the hell?*

Still, we keep playing, and then Rob arrives at the bar as well. It takes a good twenty minutes before he drags himself through the cheering crowds towards us.

Then Rob and all the hockey guys start talking with Four until one of Rob's teammates comes to whisper something into his ear. Rob's face lights up, and he even smiles when he replies, "A bet? Who did? Paige?"

He then shakes off the hands of this blond girl, who was trying to lean on him, and starts walking to the bar. *I knew it. He totally likes Paige.*

I look at Four and point out, "Did I call it or what?"

"I guess we'll see," he says, unenthused. He grabs my hand and leads our way back to the bar. I feel the anger spike within him again. *Why does he hate her so much?*

The rest of our date is spent at the bar, speaking to Paige, but I don't mind at all.

She is smart and funny, and even I would date her. Plus, Rob is definitely interested in her. They obviously have this vibe going, and he is planning to go back to her apartment with her once her shift is over.

They are a total match. I knew it.

"Can we come too?" Four asks suddenly, and I can feel the nervousness within her for a second, but she smiles and says, "Sure."

Of course, she didn't want us to come.

Once she locked up the bar, we headed over to her car, an older looking Porsche Taycan, parked at the back. Rob and I got into the back and let Four sit at the front in the passenger seat.

Four energy is now beyond nervous. Though Paige seems confident behind the wheel and even halfway drunk Rob commented on that with, "There is something sexy about a girl driving a stick."

"Nice ride," he then added before asking, "Are you rich or something?"

"I wish," she says, but it's already obvious Rob will not let her off that easily, so she adds, "I took care of someone when I was young and homeless. He was a drug addict, and when he passed, I learned he put my name on the title. It is a nice car but thank God it's not worth stealing." She smiled at that, but I don't think any of us missed the way her eye browsed over to Four.

Rob reacted, "Oh, I forgot. You guys don't like each other. Why? What happened after I left the bar? Did he hit you with a dart or something?"

"No, the game just got boring, but okay, I think this is enough," Paige added and pulled over so fast and suddenly that it made even Rob shut up for a second.

Then she turned to Four, "You have been eying me this whole time. Do you want to drive?" she added nicely, and Four was already getting out of the car. It changed then from a hummingbird under Paige's hands into a revving maniac when abused by Four. I was clutching the seatbelt in my fist as if it could help me in case of a crash.

Finally, we made it to Paige's apartment unharmed. Her place is nice but not as girly as I would expect from how she looked tonight. She also seems to know a lot about hockey, and because of that, Rob is clearly attracted to her even more.

Only Four is still acting weird and literally snooping around her apartment, but perhaps it's not that personal, as he has been on the edge for the last few days anyway. It might be because he is sober. It is the condition given by Rob for allowing him to be with me and not killing him. I feel like Four is all over the place. His energy is switching from hating Paige to hating himself, feeling guilt, anger, and most definitely confusion.

When we left Paige's place, we dropped Rob off at his apartment. He was a bit drunk and not happy that he didn't get to stay at Paige's alone with her.

He's been calling us cockblockers the whole ride, knowing that he is not getting Paige into his bed tonight, repeating the fact that he doesn't date, and she doesn't date either, so they can just sleep together when he is in town.

"She doesn't do that. You heard what Carly said," comes from Four before he asks tiredly, "Can we just not talk about her anymore?"

Wow. He is pissed again. Paige really plays on his nerves.

After Four delivers Rob safely to his bed, he comes back to the car and now it is just the two of us.

Four runs his fingers through the hair falling onto his forehead and I suddenly feel the weird low wave of his energy again when he offers, "We can crash over at Mike's cabin if you want."

Of course, I am in, but the end of the night didn't turn out the way I expected.

We talked for a while, smoked some more weed, and ended up having sex. Though I was already noticing how his energy changes every time that we end up together.

From the first time at the race, when we both fell into the temptation, where his physical side connected with his energy completely, which threw me into a crazy deal of orgasm, to tonight, when his passion felt almost desperate as if caught in the loop, hunting for something, and even though both of us reached the desired place eventually, I was already sure of the feeling and also my reading before the night ended.

We were both searching for something else.

Chapter Fifty

Damien – Out of the Way of the Boom

Every day seems to be the same now. We are back in the car and on the way to the Trap.

Four says something to me, but I am not listening, so he turns to Rob and comments, "You know that guy still has none of our lingo, right?"

"No, he doesn't. Not the sharpest tool in the shed, I guess," Rob says in their tongue and smiles at me the way you would at a cat trying to catch a fly behind the window glass. *Pitiful.*

"Are you going to see Paige tonight?" Four asks him meanwhile, and Rob shakes his head. "No. I went to the city last night with the guys and took the two girls back to the hotel. I don't think Paige will have me after that, but you didn't like her anyway. At her place, you were being a kind of an asshole."

"No, I wasn't."

Rob blows air out of his mouth before saying, "Oh yes, you were. Mia was reading Paige when she could and was surprised she didn't kick us all out of there because of you. She'll spit in your drink, that's for sure."

"What do you want from me? Should I go and apologize to her?"

Rob shares a quick laugh. "Definitely not. Mia said, Paige really hates you."

"Oh, I know she does. Good."

Then we arrived at the Trap, and I saw that Rob wasn't lying yesterday about getting the boat ready for tonight.

The wind is coming in already, and we are sailing after the shift, which is fantastic. I can't wait for the loaded truck to leave.

Rob then goes to the spot picked for clearcutting trees, and Four and I drag ourselves back to the place we didn't fully clean up yesterday. After about an hour of us working our asses off, some guy shows up, waving at Four from pretty far down the road.

When he finally gets to us, Four greets him by saying, "Uh oh," so maybe the guy is bad news. Four removes his protective glasses and adds, "Hey, Dex. What did I do this time?"

"Nothing," comes back from Dex before he acknowledges, "Well, we should talk though."

With that, his eyes ran over my existence, standing there, but Four waved his hand my way to point out, "No worries. He only speaks English and can't understand us."

Dex nods and starts speaking more directly, "All right then. You requested a profile check on that girl cadet. Why?"

Four makes an annoyed face, then he states, "She pissed me off."

"I bet," Dex answers with a smile, but Four looks back at him, still unenthused, and asks, "What is that supposed to mean?"

Dex scratches his nose before continuing, "Listen, how long have I watched you train the newbies? You are the best we've ever seen at the base and probably will ever see, but when cadet thirty-six got on that field and started to chase your ass, I was waiting for you to snap, and you did. No one made you tap out before or even came as close to you as she did. We have never called a medic for you until that day."

Four shakes his head, but the guy adds, "All those years, you have never drawn blood in a fight, not once, because that is not what you do. And please, don't give me the bullshit that it was an accident. I clearly saw you going for her neck. That scratch was a message. Just a reminder of who the Alpha male is. I get it, but then you wanted to know who she was. You ran the search, and that's not good. She is being watched, and I've had a long explanation to do with the elders because of you."

"Who's watching?"

Dex changes his face into a serious, troubled one before confessing, "Don. He has claimed her. She is to be his bride."

Four looked shocked. "Isn't he like seventy years old? Well, he doesn't have to worry. She is not my type."

Dex chuckles, "I think we both know she is everybody's type, but you will leave her alone from now on. We have been warned now, so she wouldn't mean only a slap on the wrist; she would mean a bullet in the head. Got it?"

"You are so dramatic. I don't need her ass, I have a girlfriend anyways," says Four; Dex slaps his back and adds, "Good. Remember that, and no more searches on her."

"Then you explain it to me. Her stats are one of the best. Why isn't she assigned? What's her story?"

"Well, you've seen her file. She's been through some dark shit in her lifetime. She was placed in foster care and bounced around from family to family. A pretty girl with difficult behavior. She got placed into a terrible situation, was beaten there, raped, then transferred into different care over here. The Dad there also tried to get into her pants; she attacked him and was kicked out of the system for good. She was fourteen and suddenly living on the streets. Applied to the base, fought for it and won the draft to the training camp. Going up through the ranks ever since. Not assigned, as nothing was suitable for her quite yet. She needs a challenge. A real challenge, as she is one of the best, just as you said."

Four briefly spreads his arms before asking, "So, what now? Don doesn't want me to train her anymore?"

Dex turns back as he is already on the way out at that point and says, "Oh yes, he wants you to train her. He just doesn't want you to fuck her."

"I wasn't planning on it," Four sends after him, but Dex only mumbles in the distance, "Yeah, sure, you weren't. Just stay away from her and make both our lives easier, would ya?"

After that, Four is pissed in the way I have never seen him before, and the trees are getting the full range of it, but I don't mind it because of it we finished an hour earlier than I thought we would.

I am super excited about the sailing, but before I step on board, Rob turns to me and says, "Hey, dude, I don't want to kill you just yet, so try to listen. We need to get on the wind, and we need to move fast, so for fuck's sake, don't get in the way of the boom, all right?" *Sure. Whatever that means, dude.*

Then we get on the water, and the boat cuts through the waves at a rapid speed. Dope.

Rob is moving around with power and confidence, and I realize how awesome it is to have a brother like this. I then got my hands on some booze, and that brought Rob back to me after a while, handing me a lifejacket while urging, "Put that on, I don't need you drowning on my watch."

"No, thanks. I think I am good," I say back, but Four turns around from the helm and adds, "Sure, you are good, but you are also very pretty, so shut the fuck up and put it on. I wanna do a bit of tacking here, and I am not jumping into the lake for your ass."

At that moment, I felt the way the sail was angled, acting to the wind. I also felt the booze working in my head, so knowing that he was about to do some "tacking," which quickly explained to me means using a zigzag motion to move the bow of the boat, left and right, through the wind to make headway, I surrendered and put on the lifejacket.

Four then went on with the announced tacking, and I started throwing up pretty much at the same time. I was happy when it ended, and my wobbly legs carried me back to the lake house. I found myself a bed to lie down on, and the I was out cold.

A light underneath the door woke me up a few hours later, so I got up and went to the kitchen where the light was coming from. Adele was there, preparing some dough, and was surprised to see me. I went over to her to see if she had something that I could sink my teeth into, but instead, for whatever reason, I leaned in and started kissing her. To my surprise, she didn't mind, and within a few minutes, I was standing back in the bedroom I had just come from, but this time, I was there with her. I felt still pretty drunk, kept kissing her, and we started to take our clothes off.

She is so gentle and smooth, tastes like heaven, and I can't get enough of her. She is telling me exactly where to touch her and what to do, and I would be an idiot if I didn't listen.

I am leading my hand between her thighs, and she opens them up for me. My fingers are going deep into her pussy while finding a rhythm she enjoys, and I am pressing my fingertips against all different parts of her inner walls whenever she wants. She is getting me off at the same time, and I feel pretty damn good.

"I am gonna grab a drink; I am parched. Do you want anything?" I asked her when our time was over, but she just shook her head. I am too lazy to look through the fridge in the kitchen for a soda or anything, so I go to the bathroom to drink out of the tap.

"Shit," I uttered right when I opened the door and saw Four standing there.

He is dressed in a bloody plastic apron and holds a butcher knife in his hand as well. A scene from an old Italian mobster movie. There is blood everywhere, with pieces of what seems like some dead animal placed on the floor tiles; the smell of it flies into my nostrils and gets me straight over to the toilet and throwing up again.

I then turn around and add towards Four and the bloody mess around him to say, "I hate when you do that."

Four smiles towards the toilet I just threw up into and said, "And I hate when you do that."

Then he quickly pointed with his hand, holding the butcher

knife at the bedroom door where Adele was probably still dozing off, and whispered, "Plus, David wouldn't like it when you did that."

"I did what?" I tried to play stupid, but he added, "Don't bother. I heard the whole show."

"What is that?" came from Adele almost at the exact moment when she showed up at the door, and Four responded with, "I hit a boar with the ambulance. It got it on the side of the head, so I had to kill it, so I guess that is what we are eating today?"

She says calmly, "Yes. We can work with that. I think Rob won't mind the roast or a stew out of it, and we freeze the rest."

Chapter Fifty-One

Mia – Finding Myself

I have texted Four again and asked him to come over when he is done at the Trap. I need to talk to him about us, as the facts of last night made me realize a few things about myself. I was astonished to feel how easily I get distracted by other energies. If Paige asked me, I would drop this God of a man, Four, and spend the night with her. As much as I love him, we are not eternal.

"What's up?" he starts cheerfully when he gets to my room and kisses me.

There is no point in holding back, so I go ahead and tell him everything while I can't believe that I am doing this, knowing that I am actually losing him. I still love him like crazy.

He then pulled me closer and wrapped his arms around me in that brotherly feel before adding, "Mia, you need to figure all that out, you know."

"You too," I say back, and he looks surprised, so I feel he should know it all. I go ahead and say, "There is this void inside of you, driving your energy to the edge, and I am not sure if there is a car, a drug, or a girl in this world that can fill that."

That only lights up his handsome face when he says, "I am an adrenaline junkie, you know that."

I smile at the obvious and say, "Yes, but there is something more you are searching for, so go find it because it isn't me."

"But I love you, and you know that as well, right?" he asks, but that is really not a question, so I confirm, "I know, and I love you too."

Chapter Fifty-Two

Paige – The Hockey Game

"It's a shame that Quain couldn't make it. He had to work," Mia says, and I don't know who the heck she is talking about, but I only hope she is not trying to set me up with somebody.

She kept looking towards the ice when I asked, "Who?" but she didn't hear me, as her brother had just gotten tripped on the ice, and the crowd went into a rage of disapproval.

The whistle goes. It's three seconds before the end of the second period, which means we will be starting the next one with a power play.

"I am going to powder my nose," Mia's ringing voice sounds again while she is already going to the restroom. I could hardly count the guys turning their heads her way when she was passing by walking up the stairs.

"I'll go with you," I say after her, following her lead as she for sure knows her way around here. She must have seen Rob playing or practicing here many times. When we get out of the stools in the restrooms, we walk over to the sinks; she unzips her over-the-shoulder pouch and finds a lip pencil in there.

"How's Four?" I asked as innocently as possible.

"He's at work tonight, saving lives, but anyway, we broke up."

"Oh, I am sorry. How come? You guys looked great together," I say the obvious aloud while rubbing soap on my hands.

She starts drawing a line around her top lip and then says, "We are both more complicated than we thought. I mean, I have been crazy about him for years. He is gorgeous and also a great guy, but he is a lot."

"I bet," I smile and wash the soap off my hands. She smiles back and whispers the following words like a secret, "He is a lot everywhere."

With that, she winked at me and then added, "I know you guys didn't click at all, but there is a different side of him when you know him better. Really."

"What is he like? I mean, hobbies and stuff?" I ask randomly, but she answers right away, "Hobbies? Well, the race."

Then I ask, "Is he a drug addict?"

"No. He does it for the race and the fun of it, but he is not a regular user." Then she asks, "Do you want to party with the team after the game?"

I think for a few seconds.

"I like Rob a lot, but I don't want to give anyone the wrong idea," I say truthfully while watching her reflection in the mirror as she keeps fixing her lips.

This girl is absolutely stunning. I am finished with my hands, and I just run them wet through my hair to calm the curls that come out of nowhere. The ice humidity may have made it happen. God knows.

"You are so beautiful. Just glowing with energy," she says suddenly, and I can't help but ask, "Energy? Glowing? What do you mean?"

Mia steps back for a bit, looking at me probingly before she feels calm enough to say, "I know it sounds crazy, but I see people's aura and feel their energy."

I nod and say, "Cool. What is yours like?"

She seems astonished. "Wow, no one has ever asked me that before. Mine is not colorful to me. Just a white type of light, nothing special, but yours is very red and strong. Though, it kind of hides away from my reading sometimes. You are protective of it."

That makes me share a sad smile, and she catches that.

"Something in the past?" she asks without holding back, reminding me of her brother.

I nod, but thankfully, she doesn't ask any more questions. We returned to our seats, and the third period started within a few seconds. The game is fast, with a lot of action; Rob scores the winning goal, but something within me keeps saying I shouldn't be here.

After the players ended their handshakes, Rob skated over to the board in front of us and gave me a knuckle bump through the glass. Trinity asked him to stay there for a second and took a selfie of us. Within another second or two, she sent the picture to us all, including Four. *What the actual fuck?*

If she had asked me again, I would have said at that moment, *"Mia, that is exactly why I don't use my phone."*

After the game, I was heading home.

I saw Four leaning onto the ambulance parked in front of my apartment way before I entered our building complex.

He walks up to me when I step out of my car, growling, "Okay, Boot, you proved your point. My friends like you, so now what? If this is just to get back at me, then fucking take me!"

With the last words, he stopped walking, but only a second before he would have crashed into me, and I felt the anger heat pumping within him. *I can safely say that he didn't like the selfie from the game.*

His body is overwhelming, and I would try to pull back, but my car is right behind me, so there is nowhere to go.

"This is not about you," I lie, but he moves his face closer to me and responds with a question that sounds somehow helpless. "Really? Is it not? Then, what is this?"

With that, he points to the air space between us. I hear his frustration and feel the same, but I don't want to admit it to him. I feel somehow weak in my knees when I breathe out the lie that is obvious to us both. "There is nothing."

At that, his body starts leaning in, and his minty chocolate breath lands on my lips before he adds, "Nothing? Okay. Then, stop me."

And I know I can't. Instead, I yank him closer. It all happens faster than I would have imagined, and his lips are on mine.

He is pulling me in as if he meant to crash me, his tongue working fast and hungry. I was already touching his six-pack underneath his EMT uniform when his left hand reached behind my top and found my breast. His hand touches me softly, and I am melting under it irrevocably. I am about to tell him we probably shouldn't take it further while standing on the street, but before I can push myself into leaving his tongue for a second, he receives a call.

I hear at least three rings before he forces himself to leave my mouth to say, "Shit," and then he answers the phone call. He speaks to the dispatcher for a few seconds, requesting more info on the emergency he must drive to while I get back to my senses. *What have I done again? Sigh.*

"I have to go," he said, but I was already walking toward my apartment when he added, "Boot?"

I turn around because I am too shaky to argue with him right now about calling me that, and he says, "Was that *nothing* enough for you?"

Wow. Here we go again. That arrogant bastard. Who does he think he is? Okay, he proved his point. I want him every time he shows up, but he is lucky to be driving his ambulance away now because I am ready. Ready for the war that he wanted.

Chapter Fifty-Three

Paige – The Airsoft

I have already packed up my comfortable clothes because I have decided. I will give it a try. I have seen the Airsoft flyers around the city for a while now.

When I looked it up, I found that Airsoft is pretty much like paintball but more of a military simulation where the players participate in mock combat with military-style weapons. That seems like fun.

I have a day off and I am bored, so why not. Even though the arena might just be full of kids.

Though, when I get there, I don't see any kids. Everything is taken quite seriously, as I am given the outfit and the gun right at the gate. I am also told to put a mask on before stepping out of the car. *Fine.*

The mask is dope, makes me see comfortably, and I love the rainbow reflection shield on it. I suit up and then get out of the car.

I see approximately thirty people standing by this huge field, which looks like it was literally sprinkled from above with bales of straw. Most are two meters long from all sides, but a few are smaller. They lie on each other, some creating tunnels, some leaning on the edges and offering hiding spaces around and underneath them. *Dope.*

I also see a forest in the distance behind an old farmhouse and a barn, which looks like a second level of the game.

This is going to be fun. I can't wait. So, what's the hold-up?

All the other players seem calmer than me, just waiting patiently.

Am I missing something? What is it?

Then, finally, I heard the whisper of the guy next to me announcing, "The commander is here."

The commander? What the heck? That's what the Pollwest calls their leaders. Shit. I am between the enemy. Well, that's okay. I will get myself hit fast and get out of here.

But that idea didn't go along with my temper once the game began. I started to clean them out one by one, exactly like their commander did on the other side.

Now, it is getting dark and more difficult. My shield is all foggy no matter what I do, but through the itchiness of my eyes, I spot the flags on the fence showing only two players left in the game. *Come on, then.*

I try to remain calm, but patience has never been one of my strengths. *That could get you hit, focus, you fool. You are the hunter, so get your head back in the game.*

I then lean onto the bale, letting everything else out of my mind. Only focusing and slowing my breathing enough for at least the mask to stop fogging as much.

Now. I decided. I will run out of the tunnel and make a flip. By doing that, I might have a chance to spot where the other player is.

I start running. I reach the exit and jump, but while making the flip, a body flies over me. The other player must have jumped off the tunnel I was hiding in when I charged out. I shoot, but he does as well. I am hit, but so is he.

We both get up on our feet. He throws the gun on the ground angrily, and I do the same.

He is now stepping away from me almost to the edge of the forest, but then he stops and makes the palm-beckoning move that always gets my blood going. *Oh no, he shouldn't have.*

I can already feel it.

The build-up within me.

My pulse is hitting me faster; anger is coming to the surface, and there is no taking it back.

I don't hesitate and charge at him with such a rage that I have never attacked anyone before. Still, he is very good and moves around my hits smoothly most of the time, which gets me thinking.

After fighting and being around the same body a couple of

times, one starts to see the similarity in posture, moves, and body language. The fact hits me over the head like a frying pan. I know who this is. The beckoning move was just a tease but not a coincidence. This is my leader.

Now, I managed to place a few hits into his shoulder. We both know I am charging for the same spot to send him a message. I want to mark him.

He might be working here undercover or on both sides; who cares right now? I gather all the strength that I have left at this point and hustle into his body.

We are now rolling on the ground, and he is making it evident that he also recognized me by going for the same move he scratched my neck with the last time. *Nice try.*

I get out of his grasp enough to be able to roll on the side a bit, and then I hit him under his ribs. He throws me off of him. I am back on my feet, and it's now or never.

I attack, and he steps back, covering my hits, but then trips over a smaller barrel standing in the field, which I am sure shouldn't have been there.

The leader landed on it, and as I was still in my range of attacks and did not have the best balance beneath my feet, he easily pulled me on him. The barrel bursts open under the weight of both our bodies, and a massive stream of blue ink is spilled all around, and we are rolling in the middle of it.

In the corner of my eye, I see the words on the barrel: "non-washable." Great, and as a reminder that I should focus right now, the leader hits me on the side of my neck.

"Commander, are you still in? They are closing the place," says a voice behind us, interrupting our clash. We both get up. We just stay within the move, catching our breaths, but the leader lifts his palms up, and I nod. We both know this is now over.

He grabs his gun from the ground and then turns back to face me. I stop and look at him. He points his index at me before changing it into a thumb-up right after. I nod because even I know that this was a decent fight.

He keeps his distance when we leave the field, and my legs shake so much that I have no idea how I will drive out of there.

It got so bad that I had to pull over after about two kilometers from that place and mentally regroup. After nearly two minutes of standing there, I heard the revving engine of a car coming in fast. *Of course. Who else would be driving like a maniac on these roads? It's him. Four.*

He flies by me, and the first thought that comes to my head is that he is probably coked out of his mind again, but I try to follow him anyway. I have never driven this fast. Still, I lost him. Well, I am not a racer.

Oh, there. I see him driving up the hill, but he'll be long gone before I get over there.

However, if I drive for another two kilometers, I will be pretty close to our base. My gym clothes are still at the back of my car; I can enter the base and train for a while.

When I get there, the guy at the front gate doesn't delay me; he just nods, and I pass by. It's Saturday night, so it's probably only him working at the base.

That also means there is no one here I could ask for equipment, so the gym is the only option for tonight. I enter but decide not to turn the lights on. The gym is lit up enough by the lights from outside; it's so empty and peaceful that way, but I keep my mask on anyway. It's a rule of the base.

I start with some push-ups but move on to the weights after that. I don't usually do them as the boys always occupy that area to show off, so this is my turn to have some fun. However, I only lay on one of the benches when I noticed a shadow of a running body on the hill outside.

I looked again through the window, and there was now more than just one. What is this? I remember an attack on our base that happened about six years ago. Two people were taken by the Pollwest, and one other cadet was accidentally killed. An attack? Is that what is happening? Must be. I see their shadows moving down the hill now and coming in fast.

I run to the door and then outside. I press myself onto the building, staying in the cover. Still, I already see a body leaning on the wall about thirty meters west of my location.

It is a man's figure, and when I get behind him, I go for a strike right away, but he stops my hand halfway as he must have seen me coming. Now I look at him. The same mask, the colored glasses. It's my leader. *What is he doing here?*

He starts signaling, and we move as he commands. We pass through the field, still unseen, but then we get behind our building and discover five men trying to open the door to our armory. I see Pollwest uniforms, and I know this will get ugly really fast.

When I jumped to the door and pressed the alarm button next to it, the leader had already started fighting. The alarm should wake the newbies who are sleeping at the barracks and also alarm the leaders.

The estimated arrival time for our backup is now five to ten minutes, so the leader and I need to survive that time. I am already being attacked and getting hit a lot. The two guys I am facing are definitely from a higher rank and physically very fit. Still, I am fighting for it.

If either my leader or I get taken or exposed, we will be kicked out of the RF base and unable to return or work for the Pollwest. Once identity is revealed, the person becomes unemployable. Unusable.

For me, it would be losing my job behind the bar, ending up homeless again, and probably sleeping with men to survive. That is why I am furious at this moment and probably broke this guy's hand and knocked the other one unconscious.

Now, there was only one guy I had to face, but my leader got him before he would approach me. I then turned to my leader to see if he was to signal the next move for us, but with that movement, I spotted the reflection of a light in the scope of a gun on the hill. It's pointing our way. It seems like it is about a meter to my left. *Oh, no! It's pointing at my leader.*

It was an instinct. I jumped in front of him and got hit in the back at the exact moment. My body landed on the leader's. He pulls me behind the building, as I can't do anything. I can't breathe. I only hear approaching cars of our backup but losing consciousness at the exact moment.

When I opened my eyes again, I found myself in that same bloody room that I was in the last time with my broken knuckles. However, the medic who is taking care of me tonight is a different person. He says, "You have been hit with a drill round only, so you'll be ok."

And with that, I remembered the pain in my back. *Shit. That hurts. It sure doesn't feel like a drill round wound.*

"You have been administered a dose of scopolamine to help us answer some questions," he says somewhere in the distance, which is now getting foggy. *Oh, the truth serum. Of course.*

Then another man enters the room. He comes to me and grabs my wrist. Yes, I have heard of those people. He is here to feel my pulse while I am answering their questions. You can cheat a lie detector, but you can hardly cheat a truth serum combined with a trained person, as I am sure this guy is.

His voice is disguised, but he doesn't have to bother with that. My senses are fucked up too much to recognize anyone. He asked me if I knew of the planned attack on the base, which I didn't. He also asked why I came to the base tonight, and I said truthfully that I wanted to train. He asked if I knew the leader would be here also, and I answered that I didn't. Then he asked if I knew leaders' identity, and I answered truthfully that I didn't, but I was shitting myself that he would ask me about my feelings for him, but thankfully, he didn't.

However, he did ask how I came about that bullet in my back, so I told him that it was an instinct when I saw the scope and felt the leader was more valuable than me. He asked me if I had any idea they were using drill rounds or life ammo while obviously trying to figure out if I was crazy enough to get myself killed. I guess the answer was clear. No, I didn't know the type of ammo, and yes, I am that crazy, but still, even though it is now apparent to us all how mentally unstable I am, I passed.

Then he told me that I would be excused from work as I needed to stay in this room for the next twenty-four hours until the drug was out of my system. *Great.*

When he leaves, it only takes a few minutes before my leader enters the room.

"Hi," I said to him stupidly; he breathed a voice changer sigh and said, "I still don't understand why you did that, but thank you."

I would have said so many things to him right now if I could, but I suspected all of this was being heard from upstairs, if not even recorded.

Otherwise, I would have asked him if he knew about the attack on our base tonight, as I know he is working on both sides. Perhaps he was placed to the Pollwest by an assignment from the RF, he can tell me. I would never betray him.

He then walks over to me. My eyes look up at the exact moment he places the worn and beaten-up bouncy ball I have left on the top of my clothes in the open locker into my hand.

"Thanks," I say, but I don't look at him. This gesture means nothing to him, but this ball has not been touched by anyone else but me for the last seven years.

As sad as it is, this ball is my childhood. My weapon, therapy, and friend, and now, the leader is somehow connected to it all.

Chapter Fifty-Four

Paige – The Bookie

I was almost through the first half of my shift when Ronnie pulled me out of the bar to say I was going to the race again tonight. Trinity is getting out of the deal, and they need a new bookie.

That is my chance of getting close to Four. Ronnie then reached to the back of his car and handed me my gun from the base, binoculars, speaker camera, chargers, voice recorder, GPS tracker, some pens, fobs, a coffee cup camera, and other stuff I will probably never use. Still, I shoved it into the bag he brought for me anyway.

"You be careful, all right?" he called after me, but I didn't look back. Then, I was being "fired" from the bar, but Steve begged me to call him from a payphone as soon as possible because he thought we needed to talk. He seemed stressed out, but I have my own shit to deal with right now.

I got the race info around six and headed over there. They left Trinity's wig and some sunglasses for me at the gate, but Ronnie already told me to bring my own, so I did.

I went through the same woman for the security check, and she actually smiled at me this time. After that, I opened the bets.

Four is the winner here. There is no real competition. Everyone is putting money on this man.

We are approaching the start time, but two cars are still missing. Perhaps neither alias Five nor Four will even make it tonight. There is a nervousness within the crowd, and all of the eyes point to the way they could come from, and then they do. They are racing over to us.

They stop about forty meters before the line, jumping out of the cars and charging at each other. Four has the music up so loud the sidewalk vibrated the second he opened the door of his car.

He is heading towards Five straight on, and for the first time, I recognize how dangerous he actually is. Plus, he obviously likes to fight.

I watch his moves as closely as possible. People start grabbing onto him in an attempt to stop him. He is furious beyond control, getting out of their arms quickly to the point of them literally ripping his T-shirt apart while trying to hold him back.

At this point, Chris is sprinting to help, but the girl Izzy turns to me and says while shaking her head, "Come on, Chris acts like Four doesn't do that every time. He has a short fuse."

At that time, alias Five is already getting back into his car. Four angrily rips off the remains of his T-shirt, and the crowd goes wild again. He flips them off with both hands while he walks backward towards his car.

And now, look at that.

Blue ink all over the length of his left arm. The exact opposite of my right arm blued by the same color from when I was rolling on the ground in ink pouring out of the barrel at the airsoft.

I felt the shockwave that just hit my whole body.

Oh, God. Four is my leader.

I can't stop shaking.

When the race ends, Mateo tries to talk to me throughout the payouts, but I can't focus on him. I can't believe this. So many things are running through my head right now. I am confused, but more than being in love with my leader, I feel angry with Four and betrayed by them both.

The person who I trusted more than anyone has just turned in front of my eyes into my enemy. The feeling shakes me to my core, and it's so strong that it's as if I was in mourning for losing someone. I've had my share of pain in the past, but this has brought up a similar feeling to the surface, and now, I hate him for it.

After the payouts, Mateo took me to my car and gave me the coordinates for the after-party.

"I hope to see you there, baby," he says to me when leaving, and I share a weak smile because calling me "a baby" wouldn't get him anywhere, even if I fancied him.

I started driving to the location, but then I saw a payphone on the side of the road. I took it as a sign. I threw a few coins into the machine, dialed the number I was given by Ronnie, and reported on Four. It takes only a minute or two of the leaders holding me on the line before I am given the order to kill.

The venue for the after-party tonight is a massive glass house on the top of a hill at the end of a small village. I walk throughout the property and talk to Tom for a while, who's working the bar outside by the pool.

He told me that Steve committed suicide and some people had come to the bar looking for me. *Shit. What is going on?*

A lot of thoughts were running through my head as I was walking back into the house, but at the same time, the crowd went loud, creating a wild frenzy.

I gaze at the house's front gate and see the people who are still wearing their masks from the race, ripping them off now. Someone is lighting fireworks from the top of the house, and the music gets louder.

Everyone knows what this means. Four has arrived.

He won the race again, of course. I see him coming in, trying to get through the crowds, but it's not easy, as people want to talk to him, be around him and touch him. He is just pushing them away to show his arrogance. He is probably still hyped up on coke. He wraps his arms around the two girls who just ran up to him.

They walked down the stairs to the pool, and the girls pushed Four onto one of the lounge chairs. One of them sat on his lap, and the other started pouring some booze into three glasses for them.

He is fully into it, not paying attention to anything else, so it is clear I won't get a better chance than this one.

Everything is on the line now; this is my life.

I head outside to my car, and I reach for my long-range shooter. The security at this place is non-existent, so no one will stop me. I am dressed in black and plan on staying out of the lights. I notice an excellent spot on the top of the back wall, so I go that way. I lay down, steady my hands, search through the scope, and there he is. My leader, well, actually, Four now.

Once I end him, I will jump back behind the wall. The people will cause chaos, so the way out is easy.

Let's calm down now and get my breathing steady. No thinking too much, just focus. Move my aim a bit higher, there, to his chest. Now look right at him, his chest, his heart, his face, his hands, his lips, his breath, his eyes. Damn, those eyes. Stop it. Just go ahead. Just fucking kill him. Okay, let's regroup and start again. I need to relax and just do it. This is my assignment; I can do it.

I move a bit to steady my shoulders; I relax my back and neck, take a deep breath, and then lean into my arm.

My breathing is steady now, but my heart is the trouble here. It is pumping too much, too fast. The push of blood coming from the veins under my collarbones all the way to my ears is almost strong enough to make me faint. *Shit.*

I can't focus like this. My hands are sweating, and my eyes are getting watery as well; damn, I am losing it.

"No. I can't do it. I can't kill him," I state the obvious out loud, and I am about to roll to the side, but at the last second, I spot Four's face. He is looking directly at me. *Fuck.*

I grab the gun and start running.

In the corner of my eye, I see him shaking the girls off him. He got up, and he is now running in my direction. *Damn it. This is not good.*

If he catches up with me, he is going to end me.

No way. If I need to go, that's okay, but not by him.

Chapter Fifty-Five

Paige – The Breaking Point

I can hear the speed of the train coming in fast from kilometers away. I am now standing fully decided, steady, and calm. I am not closing my eyes; I am not afraid.

There is no turning back for me. Come and take me. I dare you.

The train is now about twenty seconds away. Coming in at lightning speed, and I feel the wave of the cold air rushing towards me. I start to count down in my head. Seven, six, the lights are glowing on me now, the train starts honking, five, four. Whack. Another body smashes into mine and pushes me off the tracks.

I start to get my balance back, but I am still shocked, angry and confused. The train is honking while passing us by; I am trying to shake the body of the person off of me, but together with the air of the passing train, it causes both of us to trip, and now we are falling down the hill right next to the tracks.

My head hit a tree branch straight on, ouch, my shoulder hurts, another turn, I am definitely bleeding now, shit, that hurts, I am still falling.

I am trying to grab onto something, but it just made my hand rip open grabbing at a bush; I feel more blood, falling even faster;

oh God, is this ever going to end. Finally, I feel the flat ground below my back.

There is no way that I am still alive. And mainly, why am I?

I slowly turn myself to the side to try to look around.

Damn, I am in so much pain right now.

I feel the blood already making my clothes stick to my body. I try to focus on my surroundings, and I notice a small river running a few meters down. And there I see him. Four. Washing the blood off of his face.

How did he find me? He must have followed me with his car's lights off all the way from the party or something, as I didn't see anyone following me. Why did he save me? Is he here to kill me? He could have let the train do that, or does he hate me so much that he wants to be the one to do it? Okay then, as he likes to say, let's get it over with.

I stand up, all shaky, but scream at him with all the anger stored inside of me. "What are you doing here?"

His nose is bleeding heavily. His clothes are ripped and bloody from the cuts all over his body. He sniffs out some of the blood and turns to face me while bursting out, "You freaking lunatic, what is wrong with you?!"

Then he used the bottom of his T-shirt to wipe more blood

from his face, revealing his flexing abs that made me swallow hard. Then, he is already ripping off a part of his ruined shirt to wipe away even more blood. When he throws the piece of cloth away, he looks at me again and shouts, "God Damn it! Why would you do that?"

I notice the scratched and bloody knuckles on his hand when he starts walking towards me. His voice is almost growling now when he says, "Answer me, Boot!"

But I can't.

He keeps walking in my direction and gets even louder. "I command you to answer me!"

My body is weak and shaky with the pain of it all. Meanwhile, he is getting closer and more powerful with every step he takes. The muscles on his chest and arms show through the ripped T-shirt, and I know they could end me with just a couple moves.

I have fought with him so many times. I know how damn fast and strong he is, but I can't move right now. My feet feel like they are glued to the ground. His eyes are piercing through me, and his posture is simply overwhelming. I then finally breathe out the words, "Because I can't do it. Okay? I just can't."

He reacts immediately in a sharp tone, "What? What can you not do?"

He is now only two steps from me, at the perfect angle for a strike. He is reading me now; I know it. His voice is getting super impatient when he urges, "You better answer me right now. What can you not do?"

It was either my anger taking over or the desperate state within me that made me burst out, "You! I can't kill you! You are my assignment, and I just can't do it."

Now he scoffs. "Why not?" And with that, he spreads his arms wide. "There is nobody here. Go for it."

He then leans forward and reaches for me, grabbing my hand and placing an open pocket knife into my palm. Then grabs my hand, with the knife in it, pulling both towards him, pointing it at his chest, and orders, "Do it."

He's holding my hand with real strength now and forcing the knife into his skin. I already see a blood stain under the edge coming through.

With that, he demands again, "Here is your chance. Take it!"

He's leaning into the knife even more; my head starts spinning under his breath, and the heat of his body. This overwhelming, handsome sculpture that is leaning over me.

Chapter Fifty-Six

Paige – Over the Edge

"No," I cried out, throwing the knife away and forcing my lips onto his at the exact moment that he was leaning in to claim mine. Our bodies collide. My mind starts responding to the touch of his tongue and the taste I cannot resist. His hands are running down my body and I start rolling up his T-shirt. I need it off; I need to touch his skin. I push his shirt as high as I can reach but I am not as tall as he is, so he pulls it the rest of the way, up and over his head.

Oh shit. Look at the muscles on this guy. I place my cold hands on his abs and feel a little skip in his breath for a second. He is freaking gorgeous.

He hooks the bottom of my shirt with his finger and orders impatiently, "This comes off. Now."

And I am not waiting either. I quickly lift my arms up, and he slides it off me and one quick movement. Once my shirt is dropped to the ground, I grab his belt that is tight around his waist and yank him closer to me. He starts kissing me again, only stopping for his lips to mark my skin from the jawline to my collarbone.

"The way you taste, fuck, it's amazing," he says while cupping my breasts, massaging them, sending tingles through my body as his thumbs graze my nipples. His right hand then runs down below my waist and unzips my shorts. There was no struggle sliding them off as they were barely hanging on my hips anyway.

I start pushing the waistband of his pants down his legs while repeating his words back to him with a smirk, "This comes off. Now."

He starts tugging my black lace panties down to my knees, and he is smiling when saying, "Agreed."

I free myself from them while watching him shrug off his jeans and boxers that were underneath. *Oh shit, okay. Hold on now. He is bigger than I imagined him to be. This will not work.*

But how he looks at me right now while still smiling and saying, "Come here," changes everything.

I take the two steps between us without another thought because he is not just the racer chased by girls for his face and body; he is my leader. The guy that I have fallen head over heels in love with. The guy who has been patient with me so many times and who I love enough to take a bullet for. I let him pull me closer and lean into his chest.

He begins kissing me again, then one of his hands slides from my breast finding its way down between my thighs. His fingers start running there for a while before slipping between my folds. He then pushes them upwards to glide over a spot inside me that sends shock waves of pleasure throughout my body. With that he pulls them out of me lazily and then rams them back in right after. Making me take a quick breath of air.

It makes me arch my back, and my legs start shaking with each movement. His face is now strained with hunger when he grabs me by the hips, lifts me up, and presses my back against the tree standing behind me. I wrap my thighs around him tightly, trying to pull him closer, but he leans back slightly again, and with that, his tongue leaves my mouth. I feel a sense of emptiness.

He now grabs both of my wrists, lifting them up, and holding them above my head pinning them against the tree behind me. His chest moves heavily when he breathes out the words, "You sure that you want to do this?" He barely pauses before leaning down to kiss my neck but clearly still waiting for a response.

Is he kidding me right now? Maybe he can feel my body shaking and wants to back out of it. Please don't. I am freaking scared, but I want this, I do. Why is he hesitant?

"Four?"

"Yeah?" he answers while still kissing my neck, and I arch myself against him while hearing my voice bursting out, "Just fucking take me already."

He takes his grip off my hands letting them drop down, so I

place them around the back of his neck. Then he grabs my hips again, and pushes himself up against my entrance, then slowly in with just the tip. I gasped for air while grabbing hold of his shoulders. His tongue starts sliding into my mouth again, but his hips don't move any closer. Thank God. He is waiting for me to warm up to it a bit.

It takes me a few seconds, but then I start to push my body very slowly against him. Four reacts to it and starts stretching his way in. After a few thrusts, I feel a flutter of pleasure inside me, but I am still scared to push against him any further. He is moving faster now, sending shockwaves of pleasure through my body, and I think this must be it. I must be on the verge of meeting the edge already.

Okay, this is fine. I think I am ready. It's like he could feel it building, so he slowed the rhythm down slightly. *What the heck?* He backed up a bit to my entrance, only teasing my clit, egging me while moving enough to let the urge build up but not over-boil. Just holding me at the edge. *Oh fuck, he's good at this.*

I have never been patient, there is just too much need stored within me, asking for relief. I just don't want to wait any longer. I started swirling my hips in a circular motion, chasing after him, trying to have more of him inside me. Then, all of a sudden, I felt an internal wave wash over me so powerful that it basically scared me.

"You are so freaking beautiful," Four mumbles. I noticed the beads of sweat trickling down my back right before another wave flooded its way in, and it was so powerful that my consciousness slapped me back. *Oh no. That feels like too much. Whatever this is, I am keeping that inside.*

I pull back and try to hold out, but Four's tongue leaves my mouth with a breath of a smile. He chuckles, "No way," and with that, he plunged his cock inside, filling me and yes, he is massive. I tried not to tense up, but he must have felt me tighten up as he paused and asked, "You alright?"

"Yeah," I breathed out, trying to relax the muscles inside to take him in. Four starts moving slowly at first but then faster, still stretching me to the point of pain but now even more of a pleasure, which raises the heat of the boiling blood within me again. If I thought the previous wave was too much, then I honestly had no idea what was coming. He is now moving fast, and I feel him literally everywhere.

I am gasping for air between each thrust of his cock driving into me, taking me to the edge again. Four then breathes out, "Cum for me," and his voice literally throws me over. He's pumping in and out of me now pressing onto my back inner walls, hitting all sorts of pressure points like revving an engine. I want to scream as I feel the rush that is coming now feeling like a fucking hurricane.

"Four. I feel. I am gonna," I am getting out scattered; his

tongue continues the journey down my neck at that point when he says, "Just let go." At that exact moment, he moves his hand back down my stomach and starts running his thumb over my clit. Another five of his thrusts, and my world shivers into the waves of pleasure crashing into my ears, and there is no way of stopping it now.

My body starts thrashing around. Four grabs and holds my waist steady, but the sways of my spasm are squeezing him from all sides and pulling him in with me. I rocked my hips to meet every inch of him, and while tightening around him, I felt the moment coming; he arched himself and finally came inside me.

We then both dropped to the ground, breathless.

"That was unreal," he says after a while, still breathing fast, but I stay still. Speechless. I just can't believe this has happened to me.

I've never felt this way about someone before. I have never been this happy.

"Are you ok?" I hear him asking and realize he wiped tears off my face before adding, "Every time I have you in my arms, you cry. We need to change that."

I sniffle a little bit and ask, "What?"

"When I came to the foster at Merfolk's, I picked you up from the floor, remember?"

"That was you?" I ask, entirely shocked, and he kisses my forehead. "Yeah, and I think I have been searching for you ever since."

I face him and ask, "And what do we do now?"

Four moves over to face me fully, and he smiles, adding, "Well, if you are done trying to kill me, I have an apartment in the city that I use for training and no one knows about, so we can go there and clean up." *Sure. Let's do it.*

Chapter Fifty-Seven
Paige – The Apartment

I am confused and desperately trying to understand myself while my body is already aching again for Four. He is holding my hand on the way up back to the car, and I am literally shaking. He thinks I am just cold and says, "I'll get the heat going in the car to warm you up."

We then found his Ford Mustang parked not that far from us, and Four opened the passenger door for me then moved the seat back a bit so I didn't have to bend my hurt knee while getting in.

He then starts the engine and takes us down the road. I try not to smile but can't help it. I am satisfied and happy, but I wouldn't refuse him if he were to pull over and want another round. *Geez, what has he done to me? I am literally taking his clothes off with my eyes as I watch him drive.*

I quickly gazed out the window to ensure he wouldn't spot me staring. After all, this is my leader. I know the skills behind this guy, so he can probably read me as easily as the scan at our front gate.

"Regrets?" Four asks suddenly, and the question surprises me, so I ask, "About what?"

"Not killing me back there, when you had the chance," he answers.

I smile at first but then say firmly, "No."

With that, Four changed the gear, and the car increased the speed even more. This Mustang seems to be born for it, but I feel any vehicle would change into a race car under this guy's hands. Then Four looks at me briefly and asks, "About the sex then?

"Definitely no regrets there," I say quietly because, firstly, such a question was way out of my comfort zone. Secondly, I think it was pretty obvious that I liked it when my orgasm squeezed the shit out of him, so I turned it around with, "And you?

Four answers immediately, "I am at your service. Sign me up. Anytime."

After that, he sniffs a little bit, and the memory of the blood pouring out of his nose about half an hour ago crawls back before he adds, "I wanted to do that for some time now."

Oh, here we go. Is that really why he pushed me off the tracks just a second before the train took me? He just wanted to add me to his body count. Well, he can scratch that off his list as accomplished.

Four changes gear and continues, "If I wasn't dating someone else at that time and Damien wasn't hanging down the frozen hole, I would have tried to take the red lacy string off of you back at the caves." He smiles and chuckles, "You kept me up all night."

Interesting. I thought he hated me.

"I did?"

"Yes, and it was hard not to say anything when I saw you at the base. I also wanted to go after Knox, but my cover would have been blown. He has been sniffing around me for months."

"And how long have you known about me?"

"First, I only thought of it with the keys at the race, but then I was sure when you snatched the shot glass at the bar. Your hand eye coordination is too good not to be noticed. I've seen such a skill only once with a cadet that we have at our base. I had to know if it's you, so I requested a check on your file," he answers.

So, he saw my file. He knows my past. He knows how damaged and crazy I am. He knows that I was looking through the scope tonight, wanting to kill him, and still, he decided to push me off the tracks, kiss me and fuck me.

Four looks at me briefly again and asks, "And when did you realize it was me?"

I think back a bit and say, "The airsoft game."

Four nods, and I add, "There, I knew that my leader and the Pollwest commander were the same person." I then smiled at my words, adding, "But it all changed when I saw the blue ink on you."

I must have put some tone into the last word as he reacted immediately, "I wanted you to hate me. It was the only thing holding me back from doing something stupid, which would expose us both."

At that point, Four grabbed my hand briefly and then went quiet. Just running through his thoughts when we were already passing through the gate to the underground parking of his apartment building.

His place smells nice. A combination of wood and leather, and he obviously turned this huge studio into a gym.

Four walks to the kitchen corner and hands me a drink from the fridge. He opens one for himself and takes a sip. My shaky legs bring me to the window, and I place the bottle on the windowsill. I look around and say, "Nice place, I like it."

Four nods while I read from one of the diplomas hanging on the wall. "Quain Thomas Zeller."

"Quain," he corrects before taking another sip from the bottle and then explains, "The family I was placed with changed my papers into Quain Thomas at some point, but I have always been only Quain. Named after my Dad. But everyone calls me Four anyways. I like it better."

"It suits you," I say to fill in the time, but then our eyes meet again. We are both searching through and beyond that look before he points at my knee with the bottle he still holds and states, "That needs to be cleaned up."

I look at where he points and see blood dripping down my

shin. I bend over quickly and try to wipe it with my hand before it drops on the floor, but that way, I don't see him walking over to me, so it surprises me when I am suddenly lifted up and carried away.

Four lands me back on my feet next to the shower, pointing to where the towel hangs.

"Call me if you need anything," Four says while turning away, but I reach for his hand and stop him from walking out. He follows my pull, and his lips crush mine at first, but then his hands run through my hair, turning it all into a soft touch. The feeling is powerful and overwhelming.

His hands gently move along my shoulders and my back, sending shivers through my spine while I run mine over his arms, chest, exploring his body once again. Our kiss isn't urgent, as in the forest, it's softer, sweeter this time.

We are now connecting with a different passion. It is run by the deep-seated need to be found. There is nobody else on Earth but Four who could understand the amount of insanity in me and the amount of pain. It is the same urge that gets him into racing and gets me into jumping off the cliff now and then.

Then we step into the shower together, and he turns on the water, so we let the warm spray win over the memories of the whole day. Between his kisses and the touch of his hands, I feel amazing. Four starts cleaning the blood from my knee, he is so gentle, touching me in a way that no one ever has before and both of my legs begin to shake.

"I am sorry," Four says, thinking the tremble is a result of the pain of the messed-up knee, so I bend down to him, shake my head with a smile, and run the top of my fingers down his jawline. He stands up while my gaze stays locked in his; he gently grabs the side of my neck and pulls me closer. Our lips meet again, and his tongue slides slowly between my lips at first before delving deep into my mouth to find me. I let out a soft moan when leaning into the kiss, wanting to get more of him, and now, I feel his hunger.

He is pulling me in, breathing faster and getting lost in the moment. I push him into the wall behind him, but then he suddenly stops as if he had gotten slapped. He pulls back, so I look at him, confused.

He holds me away from his body at arm's length and breathes heavily before saying, "You are hurt, so we should chill because I can't take much more of this. I won't be able to stop if we keep going."

"I don't want to stop," I fess up before pushing him down to the floor and gyrating my hips over him. I don't know how I was planning to do this as he is so freaking big, but the way we are right now reminds me of the time on the top of a cave, so I say jokingly, "One, go, and we are pulling on go, okay, Boot?"

He really smiles now, grabs my hips, and lifts me up so he can start easing his way through my entrance, and I can't imagine anything more beautiful than the sight of him right now. He is looking into my eyes while still gently holding my hips. Shit. I just got reminded of his size when my muscles stiffen tight around his shaft.

I tingle all over but then awaken from the first shock, I am starting to like it again and a lot. I give myself up to his size that he is now pushing into me, hitting a spot I never knew existed while his hand finds my already swollen clit. He begins to work on that bundle of nerves at the same time.

I start chasing the friction of his fingers, and my hips keep following the rhythm until the pleasure rolls through me again. My walls flexing and fluttering around his cock while pulling him into the blissful escape with me.

After we landed down from the high of our orgasms, he shook his head and said with a surprisingly bitter tone, "Shit. I knew it. I am so sorry."

I looked where he was pointing and saw a blood puddle underneath my knee before he regretfully said out loud, "You are bleeding again, we need to get it bandaged up."

And before I manage to say that it actually seems worse than it feels, as the water multiplies the look of the blood, I am already wrapped in a towel and being carried out of the bathroom.

"There is no bed in this place, as I don't sleep here," Four states apologetically but adds, "I have some blankets though."

He then brings them over together with the first aid kit, and it is obvious he spent a lot of time around paramedics as I am soon very professionally patched up. He found two sets of T-shirt's and sweatpants for us both.

I keep watching him and wondering. Why can't I take my eyes off of this man?

Because of the way he moves around me with the same dominance that he brought to every training we spent together. Because it all has now changed into a soft touch. Because of the sense of his sexual power and the look of this T-shirt stretched across his broad shoulders and chest. The way his messy hair is half wet from the shower almost covering his blue piercing eyes, his handsome face that no one else can compare to, his low-hanging sweatpants glamorizing the V-shaped body, because of his minty chocolate breath and mainly, because I am in love with him.

We then lie together on one of the training mats. I miss his touch, so I move closer and lean my temple on his bicep. It just feels right.

The room is only lit up by the streetlights from outside, just enough for us to see our silhouettes.

I hear him breathe a smile when I run my finger gently over the top of his nose, which has been bleeding so much tonight. Still, his breathing stops completely when I trail my hand down to his six-pack and below.

"I want you again," I whisper; he runs his hand over mine and says, "Oh, hell, I want you too, but don't you need to get some rest?"

"No," I say, lean in, and demand the touch of his tongue again.

When I stopped playing with him, he smiled, and while rolling his body on the top of mine, he added, "I knew you'd be the end of me. The second I saw you in that bar, I freaking knew it."

And with that, he becomes a part of me again, and my body is a fragment of his without anything but a trust between us. He is giving himself to me, and I have lost control over my own body the second he laid his mouth and hands on me.

I found myself back in reality again, with my legs tightened around his hips, holding him inside of me while he was pumping the waves of my fourth orgasm. I don't think even he could squeeze another one out of me tonight. In a good way, but I am exhausted.

I left his apartment in the morning with shaky knees, seeing him sleeping on the mat. I knew with my whole being that I would destroy, kill, and hunt beyond eternity anyone who would try to hurt this man.

I get into the cab I called, and the driver is looking at me probingly on the way as if reading me or something.

He then suddenly stops the car, looks back at me again, and asks, "Did you kill him? I hope not," and with that, he points a gun at me and shoots.

Chapter Fifty-Eight

Paige – A Wakeup Call

My mouth feels so dry and I am not liking the feeling of the nasty bag placed over my head. I hate the dark but if I tilt my head a bit, maybe there is a chance of seeing something.

"Don't make any moves," says a voice somewhere to my left. It is a voice that I don't recognize. He adds, "I am ordered to pump more into you if you do."

Okay then. That complicates things. I go back to just sitting there. Sweating and waiting. I should feel desperate, but I don't.

Even though I still feel dizzy from whatever drug was used on me to bring me here, my hands are not tied, and they are one of my strengths. Still, who knows if there'd be any chance of even using them. I will try to make the guy speak again. I must figure out the angle and distance between us.

Before I have a chance to try anything though, I hear footsteps coming my way. A door opens, someone walks through and then says, "You can take it off now."

I rip the bag off of my head, seeing Don and his two bodyguards standing there in front of me.

Don pulls out a chair from the table, sits down close to me, and recites into my face, "Hi, honey. Welcome home. We are getting married."

I look back at him, but before saying anything nasty to his creepy face, I spot the bodyguard behind him lifting the tranquilizer gun again. *They all suspect me. I better play this smart. I have to bullshit them.*

I smile back and say, "Well, it took you long enough."

"I knew it," he shouts out and seems happy with himself, "Just playing the game. You are my green-eyed jewel. I will have you covered in diamonds. You will be so happy that you are mine."

I pretend to smile again and be as lovely as possible when asking, "So, what about my assignment?"

"Oh, Four? He cut a deal with both sides. He called in only a few minutes after you had been assigned and ordered to end him. He has people working for him everywhere. He was told not to go to the race after party as you would be there waiting for him, but he went anyway. That's his arrogance but they were actually shitting themselves thinking that you would in fact kill him at the apartment," he says while taking the toothpick out of his mouth for a second before looking at my cut up sore knee and adding, "I see you fought him, but he didn't touch you otherwise, did he?"

I can't even think about what body part of mine Four didn't touch last night but I definitely can't say that to Don.

"No, he didn't," I say to make him happy, but another fact

hits me by what Don said. Four cut a deal with both agencies, so the only person exposed here is me, and my only way of any future is by marrying Don at this point.

Don then grabbed me by the hand, and we were walking out of the basement together. We start going up a tall staircase which takes us into a huge room with the most beautiful chandelier, then we continue on up the stairs to the second floor. Don leads me into one of the rooms that is to be mine apparently.

I spot a window, and Don comments on the view right away. "Yes, it's an island. We are staying here until the wedding."

Okay then, I am screwed.

I feel my anger pulsing its way through my veins all the way to my head giving me a headache. I am back where I started seven years ago. Feeling hopeless.

Back with the boys in foster, pushing me into the corner to touch my breasts and other places for fun, back on the floor, after being raped, back in the training, trying to prove myself, hours of sweat, blood, and tears, fighting with everything until the final tap and for what?

What am I doing here? This can't be happening to me!

Meanwhile Don keeps speaking but I am withdrawn from it. I only registered that he said he will have to fly out for a day or two and meanwhile I need to get the shopping list of my wedding stuff ready, so we can have it delivered. He then places a small kiss onto my lips. I try not to pull away but want to with every ouch of my being. *Ew.*

Soon after that Don and his bodyguards leave the room, and I am running through my options in my head.

The first thing I must do is check out the security of this place. I change into some clothes I found in the dresser, and I walk over to the front terrace of the house.

I then start pretending to stretch and do some yoga while looking around and counting security cameras on the roof. Then I go down to the beach for a run while checking out the fences, the gate and waving goodbye to Don leaving in his helicopter.

After the helicopter is out of sight, I don't wait for anything. I dive into the water. The current is quite strong and the water cold. *Where am I?*

I drive down deep but when I swim back up to the surface to take a breath, I hear the sound of a helicopter approaching.

Don must be back already. There's no way. That soon? Crap.

So, I pull myself above the water again after a while but instead of Don, I see a line-up of people standing on the beach, waiting for me. There is nowhere else to go, so I start slowly swimming back to the shore and then begin walking out of the water.

"All this fuzz for one girl," the guy, who must be a leader of them, says my way when I get closer.

I see his eyes in the mask, checking me out, when he is stating, "But I get it now. The eye does not go wanting."

I know the type of masks they are all wearing. Is this the RF? Perhaps a mission to rescue me?

The guy then points towards the bruise on my face and asks, "Did they do that to you?"

I don't respond. He points towards the helicopter and says "Get in." I look around but there are just too many of them to make it worth trying anything to get away, so I hop in.

The flight was not long and at least no one put a bag over my head this time.

Once we land, I am taken to an interrogation room with just a table and two chairs in it and I am asked to sit down on one of them. *What is going on?*

In the room there is a light hanging from the ceiling right above my head now that is obnoxiously bright which makes it very hard to see what's going on past the glass door. I hear people but only see their figures moving by.

The voice of the guy who brought me here speaks to another person behind the door, but I only catch the ending, "someone worked her over, but she won't tell."

Then they enter the room, and the body of the other person moves to the left with a manner that I know too well at this point. Bringing in the same power and control, as when moving over to the elevator in the bar the first time I saw him and the same way he entered the field at the base as my leader. There he is. All masked up but unable to hide from me anymore. It's Four.

"Take her to the base. I want eyes on her until the end," he says.

Really? Are we back to that? Not even six hours ago I still had his cock in my mouth, but I get it. Why should I matter more to him than any other one-night stand? I'll manage.

Four leaves the room and then someone grabs my arm. I get up and follow the person whose build seems quite skinny and young.

We walk out of the room, and I notice another figure walking behind me. That one is heavier set and I noticed dark eyes through his mask when I looked back quickly. A gun hangs on his left side.

We are then entering what seems to be an underground loading dock where I am then pushed into the back of a van. I realize then that I am most definitely dealing with cadets and probably even newbies. As, if I were to ask to escort someone, I would never put him or her at the back of a vehicle, with armed company and loose hands.

I almost find it insulting.

We get on the road and the young one starts smiling at me. *Is this some kind of a joke?*

His gun is not secured and fully exposed to my eyes, the way he is leaning on the window means that he favors his right, and he is also wearing a rope necklace for fuck sake.

So, I let the show go on for about five kilometers and when we approached the tree covers of the forest I had just about enough.

I jump on my feet and charge for the guy's left. He looks so shocked when he sees his gun in my hands that he screams which makes the driver turn his head our way and he forgets to pay attention to the road.

The van then hits the curb at full speed, and now we are rolling. I am trying to grab a hold of something but with the next flip, my back hits the back door, I hear a crack behind me, the door opens, and I am flying out.

My body falls into a ditch, just a few meters from a tree. Lucky that I didn't hit the tree but also not, because I am breathless and the sharp pain in my chest is almost enough to make me faint. I try to take small sips of air, but my lungs are fighting me back even on that.

Damn, that hurts.

I stopped forcing it, closed my eyes and surrendered to the ground.

It's a weird dream in my head now. The sound of wings flapping in the air gets louder and louder then suddenly I am awake. My eyes open, and I spot a huge bird landing into the nearby trees. Shoot, now I remember what just happened. I freaking just flew out of the moving car.

And that is not even the worst thing that just happened. My escape window is closing up on me while I am still almost breathless and that's a real problem. One of the guys in the van in the distance on the road is speaking to the other and that reminder makes me move my hurting body again. I push myself to the edge of that grassy level of the hill, I start slowly rolling down but along the way the pain takes over and I pass out again.

When I wake up, it almost feels like late afternoon but at least my nose stopped bleeding and I can breathe without as much pain. *Let's try to move again.*

I get up slowly, but the pain takes me down to my knees. I stayed there for a few minutes, just breathing through the pain and standing my body up a little bit at the time.

Now, let's get my head back into the game. What am I to do next?

First, I need to change clothes because I am literally freezing and second, I need to get my hands on a gun.

There. I see lights down below this hill on the left side of the shore.

It looks like a logging place of some sort. Those sites definitely keep food, clothes and most likely guns.

Chapter Fifty-Nine

Mia – Meeting Again

I hear Four's voice through the door, saying, "Hey, can I come in?"

Such a question is pointless. There is nothing I would refuse to this guy.

"Sure!" I say.

His presence always brings something with him, but his energy today is weird and makes me look at him. "Oh, no, what happened to you?

He has a black eye and the thought of him hitting an airbag straight on flashes through my head, but I don't even know if an airbag would cause such damage.

I also see scratches and bruises on other parts of his body, and I am thinking at least his elbow might need a stitch or two but at that point, he already slammed his body down onto one of my beanbag chairs laying on the floor.

His hand points to the other one, then he fully looks at me and says, "Come here. Don't worry, I am no danger to you today. I have no body fluids left in me."

I sit down next to him and run my hand through the hair lying on his forehead. I feel his beautiful energy and even as injured as he is, he is so freaking handsome, it's just crazy.

"Are you okay?" I asked but at that time I already knew he might not even have time to answer. His pager was going crazy since he said the first words at the door and the energy of it was already giving me a headache.

He grabs his phone and dials out. Then, jumps up. "A cab driver? What? Is Don behind this? Where is she?"

With those words, he is waving goodbye to me and then running down the stairs.

I realize it's time for me to go to work and get myself on the next bus to the hospital.

The shift was okay, even though I was aware of the head nurse watching my breaks and making notes of the food that I consumed. *Sure. Whatever.*

When I am back and sitting on the bus heading home, I get this feeling of guilt as it has been a while since I went for a run. Once I get home, I quickly change into my workout clothes and within the next hour I am there. I am running down the shoreline.

The sun is going down slowly, and I can already feel the cool breeze in the air. *Beautiful. I love this time of day.*

I was almost at our lake house when I suddenly saw someone stomping out of the forest about a hundred meters from me. The aura together with the energy was only possible within the one and only. Paige.

"Hi," I say when I get over to her, she nods, and I feel her heart pumping her energy even higher than the last time I saw her. *Breathtaking.*

Her skin is only lightly tanned but her green eyes are pulsing out of her face once again like two emeralds and I can't stop staring at them.

Paige must have been running for a while though, now I finally start paying attention to the whole picture and notice a bunch of injuries on her body. Almost at the same second, a sound of a helicopter comes through the clouds somewhere above the mountain, and it is heading our direction. Paige smiles at that and admits, "Yep. I am in trouble."

"Our house is over there, come on!" I called back at her because I was already running that way waving her on to follow me.

She did, and when we got into the kitchen of the lake house, she asked me to pretend that I am cooking something as the people from the helicopter will most likely be scoping the place and they can't find anything weird about me being here. I do as she says, and the wind whipping noise passes by the house as I am cutting into the first onion.

Then I can't help but ask, "Why are they after you?"

"An old guy wants me to marry him, and the other one would like to kill me, I think," she states while hiding behind the curtain next to the window. I am reading her energy as it is within my reach now, so I can feel that she is telling the truth. Though, there is more behind it but who cares? She is here and I am glad she is safe now.

She asked, "Would you mind if I grab a few supplies?" So, we began to walk through the house together and her eyes spotted a few things that she needed.

"That's Four's but I am sure he has others, plus he is super busy at work and doesn't come here that often anymore," I commented towards the gun she grabbed from the corner of the attic. She then said that we need to mess the place up a bit to look like someone broke in and took it. *No problem, I guess we can do that.*

I showed her where the keys were for the house so she could always come back, but she said she would be using the window at the attic if she was to come in. She asked if I could leave it unlocked.

I wouldn't even look up at the attic window without my head spinning but she obviously won't have issues with using it to come in. Once again, she continues to take my breath away.

I ask if I can help with anything else because I just wanted to be near her as much as I can. At first, she is not keen on pulling me into her troubles but when I won't let it go, she nods and gives me more info.

Once we talk for a while, I head out and get on the bus to the city and walk to the address that she has given me. I headed up to her apartment to grab the things she asked for. Pretty much the whole bathroom cabinet, plus hair coloring, brown contact lenses, a pair of runners, and a towel.

Once I get back to her with everything, I see her pulling money out of one of the shoes, some pills out of her box of tampons, and a black USB stick.

I keep watching her breathlessly. She has this magnetic pull on me, and I feel almost addicted to her. I am now looking at her body, her eyes, her lips, and out of nowhere, I go over to her and press my lips on hers.

After a second or two I move away and see her confusion. I am desperately trying to read her energy, but I get nothing. That protective shield is back. She smiles and says, "You are beautiful Mia, but I am sorry I am not into girls."

Chapter Sixty

Damien – Baked

We are laying on the floor in the living room, Rob throws away the pillow covering his head and asks, "Hey, did you crash again?"

Four's eyes browse over the wounds on his body that I noticed like fifteen times already as he looks seriously beaten up and says, "Oh, that. Right. I crashed into someone. The best night of my life, if you know what I mean."

Rob looks at him again and states, "No, I don't. You hit your head more than you think. You should have that checked out."

Four replies, "I was fighting it for so long, and now I can't get enough. It blows my mind. It's crazy."

Rob sits up, leaning closer to him with a probing look and almost whispers, "Are you high right now?"

"Nope, but it sure feels like it," says Four with a smile while already getting up from the sofa and leaving for upstairs to see Mia.

Rob turns to me. "Let's bounce."

And with that, my time for breakfast went out of the window. But before we walk through the door, Rob turns to Anna with a tired look and a question, "Does he really need to know how to do that?"

Anna nods, and Rob pulls me through the door by my shirt

to say, "All right, little buddy. Dad thinks you need to know how to cut grass with a scythe. Don't ask me how I know that this is not a good idea, no one ever does, but it was a rite of passage or some other bullshit in his ancient times, so we are doing it."

"What is a scythe?" I ask.

"Ahh it is kind of like a giant machete that you cut the grass with; you'll see."

Shit. Things are getting better and better.

After a couple of hours slamming the scythe through the grass and not getting any better at it, only designing a bunch of blisters on my hands, I am sure that Rob will beat me to death with the scythe and feed me to the bears.

This guy is on some adrenaline-dopamine combo kind of shit and has no patience whatsoever. The only reason I was still alive in the middle of this was Four, who joined us in the afternoon. He took it from him because Rob had to leave for the ice rink, and within the next thirty minutes, I was mowing like there was no tomorrow.

Four is a mentor. A born leader that can teach you anything. However, he then had to leave for some emergency. He offered to take me home, but I wanted to stay and chill.

I set myself down in the kitchen after getting baked and went through all the snacks. Suddenly, I start to hear all kinds of weird noises from the woods outside, and that is it, I am outta here.

I almost remembered the way home, so I started walking. It took about ten minutes before I admitted to myself that I was lost. Now, every single noise literally scared the shit out of me, and I am sure happy to see the lights of a cabin in front of me in the woods.

The smell of hash and some kind of chemical, like when my Mom colors her hair or something, hits me even before I knock on the door, but then someone opens and pulls me inside.

The people there started screaming at me in their language, and I just yelled back in English to the point when they stopped.

Then they all started laughing. Since I was high and had no idea what was happening, I laughed along with them. One of the guys passed me a mask, so I put it on because the smell started to burn my eyes. Almost at the exact second, the door bursts open, and the cops come running in, yelling, "Get on the ground!"

We all get taken down to the police station, where it turns out those people were cooking meth, which of course I was not actually a part of. Thankfully they didn't ask me too many questions, I think they realized pretty quickly that I had no part in it, so they told me to call someone to come pick me up. Now, I am sitting here in custody and still smiling. I am hungry and want to laugh but I try to hold it in.

It doesn't take long before the door opens, and Four walks in. He grabs me and urges, "Let's go little buddy," but before we get to his car, he takes a call, which stresses him out the way I have never seen him before.

I am still high and smiling when he's yelling back into the phone. "What? What do you mean by jump out of the van? How long ago was this? Where is she? Are the guys okay?"

Four is using his one free hand to get me into his truck, but I still feel like dancing and want to have a good time, so he grabs me more forcefully and tries to push my head down again. He's getting nervous, I can tell, even before he urges with, "For fuck's sake, dude just get in the truck."

Now I am sitting in his passenger seat and moving my head to the music that is not even playing, but I can hear it in my head loud and clear. Four sits his ass next to me and states, "My gun has gone missing from the lake house, and I think I know now where it might be."

I smile at him widely again, but he shakes his head. "No, little buddy, it's not that funny. She can have an eye on us right now. She is damn fast and doesn't hold back, so you make one wrong move, and you fly home in a casket."

I looked back at his serious face and just laughed my ass off.

Chapter Sixty-One

Paige – Free Again

After Mia left, I put some gloves on. I am not touching anything in this house without them on as I don't want my fingerprints left behind.

I went through the kitchen and found a lot of stuff in there. I cleaned up my wounds while looking at the pictures around on the walls and in frames on the table.

Evidently, Four has been Rob's friend since at least since they were in middle school. I see a lot of hockey pictures, sailing, fishing, hunting, diving with sharks, Four flying a helicopter, Damien driving a tractor, Mia in some beauty pageant, pictures of their parents, and also of some other guy who would fit for Rob's father as he looks like his double. I guess their Mom remarried.

Meanwhile, I found some scissors and gave myself a haircut. I need to look like someone else and not me, so I cut it quite short. The rest came out pretty white when I finally remembered to wash the coloring away. I dressed in the dark green stuff Mia brought from her house and got on with my search.

I knew I couldn't stay at this place for more than another hour or so. I will get it prepped but try not to return afterward. Once the gun goes missing, I am sure Four will strip the house down to its core to find it.

I get on with searching through the woods. I run a circle of five kilometers or so and find two cabins I can crash in. I chose one for tonight. The pressure is on, for sure. I had to lay down and hide a few times as the helicopter was still circling the area, but while on the run, I also spotted a sign down by the lake that said "looking for help."

The place down by the water runs a business taking tourists on a boat ride around the lake and is owned by Max and his wife, Margaret. They are in their seventies and desperate for extra hands, so I get hired the next day.

Max first goes about needing to see my license before he lets me take the boat out on the water, but then I show him how it is done, and he no longer insists. He doesn't even ask me what my name is. I pretend to stutter, so he just calls me Sport.

On Thursday, after my shift, I sit in a spare room where customers normally wait in for the boat to come pick them up, and I watch a hockey game that's playing on the TV. I am alone and enjoying the night. Rob is playing great, and I like watching him. He is fast, sees the game, and predicts others. There. He scored again.

I decided to lie down on the bench to rest while watching him and still holding the warm cup of tea in my hand when I suddenly heard the voice behind me that I would recognize anywhere. "He is amazing, isn't he?" Four asks, and I stay frozen.

Oh, no. Is he speaking to me? Does he know I am here?

"Yes, he is one of a kind. Margaret's favorite," answers Max from the counter, and then continues, "Is it Thursday already? I think Margaret still has some meds left from the last batch."

"Well, she shouldn't have," comes back from Four, and I am sure not even breathing, but he continues with the small talk. "How is business going?"

"Good, things are going well," comes back from Max. "As long as we keep it going, you know."

Then I hear them both walking out of the room and opening the back of Four's car. The door closes after a while, and the engine is back on, but I wait another ten minutes without a single move until I am confident that he is gone.

Meanwhile, Max returned behind the counter and spotted me. "Oh, there you are, Sport. I wanted to introduce you to someone. A very nice lad. You would like the look on him for sure."

Well, he might be right, at least about the last part.

Chapter Sixty-Two

Damien – The Bar Night

I am back sitting on the tractor and Four is taking us up to where the trees were cut down for us. Rob has a game today so it's just the two of us working and I know that I will feel it tonight for sure.

Four isn't saying much, perhaps he is pissed about covering for my little police incident or something. When we take our break, he looks through the hills with his binoculars again and there I finally ask, "Are you looking for the girl you talked about yesterday? The one who took your gun? Does she have a beef with you or something?"

He breathes out, "I guess she does."

I move my face closer to him when asking, "Is she dangerous?"

"You have no idea. The fastest hands I've ever worked with," he admits and looks super tired. I noticed he doesn't sleep over at our house anymore and from the sight of him, he probably hasn't slept at all lately.

He then grabs the hair away from his forehead when saying, "You know, it's not like she'd be the first one to try to put me in a body bag, but it would sting more. And maybe I am just making shit up in my head. I mean I see things have moved around the lake house; I see an escape route as if someone has the place prepared but then why would that be her. She probably got on the first train out of here and I will never see her again. But then, soldiers don't do that. The base is like home after seven years, you know?"

I smile and shrug my shoulders. He gets it and switches to English. "But she is more than home. She is like a family to me."

I lift my eyebrows. "Family? That wants to kill you. That'd make Christmas pretty awkward, no?"

He smiles briefly and shakes my head with his hand a bit before saying, "Rob will meet us in the city. We are going out tonight."

And you know what? I can't even argue at this point.

It's around nine in the evening when we get to the same bar that I went to with Rob the other day, and he meets us there after his game.

We start drinking and it's more than obvious that Rob is like a celebrity around here. He can have anything and any girl he wants, but he says he is sticking to his choice, whatever that means. He asks Four, "Are you not going for Tracy tonight? Are you feeling sick or something?"

"No. I am done with that, plus there is some work hassle that came up and it's a real shit, you know."

Rob takes another sip of his beer before asking, "Is that

what's keeping the copter in the air and your eye in the woods all the time?"

Four nods and Rob lifts his eyebrows again, asking, "Should we be worried?"

"No. It's just a runaway thing," Four breathes out, so Rob changes the subject. "It's crazy about Steve, isn't it?"

I start to look a bit bored at that point, so they explain to me that the owner of this bar was found dead, and tonight is kind of a life celebration party for him.

I wanted to ask about it and start a conversation but exactly at that moment I saw them both looking at the girl who parked her ass right next to me. She waves a vape in front of my eyes and whispers into my ear, "You wanna come for a smoke?"

My legs are already taking me outside when I hear Rob sending after me, "Don't do anything I wouldn't do."

We walked through the back door into an alley where we hit her dope a few times before she shoved me into some hallway and started unzipping my pants.

Later that night I told Rob about how I ran away from her, and a guaranteed blowjob and he laughed his ass off when commenting, "Yeah, dude that sounds like my Thursday afternoon."

Chapter Sixty-Three
Mia – The Doctor's Lounge

My night shift was over, and I was on my way to grab my stuff before leaving the hospital, but I was so thirsty that I decided to first make my way to the doctor's lounge to grab a soda from the vending machine.

"Good morning," comes from a young doctor sitting in one of the chairs. When he hears the noise of the falling bottle out of the soda machine, it makes him lift his eyes up from whatever he is reading.

His name is Jacob. I haven't seen him since he admitted me the day of my overdose accident. He smiles at me, and I smile back. His hand then points to the chair next to him with an invite. I know I am exhausted and want to go home, but he is too attractive to ignore right now.

I sit in the chair beside him, and his cologne hits my senses. It comes as a huge overload, bringing me an immediate headache, but I don't mind it because the pain of it keeps me from falling asleep. I am watching him. No, I am actually staring at him.

There is something about him. He has thick black hair, and straight from the first look, I catch myself thinking about how it would feel to run my hands through it. I see the skin on his neck running over his Adam's apple, creating a cute little bump. I see his orange aura and feel his energy that is coming through in irregular spikes, which are similar to Rob's a few years ago when he didn't know how to admit that he broke Dad's car window when practicing slap shots in front of our house.

That energy spike means Jacob is hesitant about something.

About a decision. What is it? Talking to me? Asking me something? Does he want me? Oh, yes. I think he wants me. Okay. He better say something now, or I am going home.

He is looking at me, and we go ahead with the typical, "How are you?" but then I smile at him again, and he says, "I haven't seen you in a while, but I heard you are being a good girl. They are keeping stats on you and saying you are doing well lately."

I see him watching my lips, so I run my tongue over the bottom one while looking straight into his eyes and respond, "I am a good girl, but only when I want to."

"Are you a good girl for someone else right now?" He says with a smirk.

I then bite my lip a little bit. *I can't believe I just said that. However, he clearly liked it.*

I shook my head to answer his question. "No, not right now," I don't understand why it is so natural to speak to him. I normally don't connect that easily with anyone.

Perhaps because he works here, and I know him from the shifts we spent together.

"Can I get your number then?" Jacob interrupts my thoughts and hands me his phone. I type my digits into it and then head for the door.

His first text came through while I was on the bus home, and the next twenty or thirty arrived throughout the next day. I agreed that I would come to his place when he got home from his shift at the hospital, and after spicy text messages back and forth, we both knew that I would be heading over there for a booty call. And an interesting one at that.

Mom was sitting on the sofa and watching a movie when I got home from Jacob's apartment in the middle of the night.

"How was your evening?" she asked, and I said it was good because it was.

However, I felt absolutely exhausted from Jacob holding me in place so that I had no choice but to take it when he fucked me hard before he tied me to his bed, teased me for almost an hour without letting me cum until he would allow it so I would be the good girl that he wanted me to be. That I will definitely not be telling my mom about, so "it was good" will have to do.

I hate to admit it, but my mind kept going between thinking

about Four and then thinking about Paige the whole night.

Then, when Jacob untied me from his bed, the feeling was finally clear as a day.

Paige and Four?

Yes, I have strong feelings for them both.

Chapter Sixty-Four

Paige – The Chase

Yesterday was my last night sleeping over at Max's boat.

I have been switching between the cabins and this place for two weeks but staying in the neighborhood and taking the risk of Four coming in unexpectedly was just too high.

Today, I gave my resignation and refused any money that Max was offering. I have enough on my accounts, plus cash hidden in other places in my apartment that is prepaid for another two months. Even though the place is definitely being watched, we were able to get Mia in and out of there once before, so we can do so again if needed.

Mia is coming with me to the city, which is excellent, and I feel at ease as hardly anyone is looking suspiciously at two girls sitting on the bus. Mia is the most beautiful girl I have ever seen and has a soft spot for me. She told me a bit more about herself, which makes me super protective of her now.

I like her a lot. When we were parting ways, I promised to keep in touch, and once I was settled in, we would go for a drink together. She gives me a kiss on the cheek before getting back on the bus, and I realize then maybe I am attracted to her. *Well, that's new. I have only ever thought about guys in that way before.*

Getting a new apartment was easier than I thought. I talked

to and showed my fake ID to the guy with a vacant studio on the east side. He said only after a few minutes of showing me around the studio that I can have it. He then gave me the keys and I paid him three months' rent. *I am off to a good start.*

I headed over to a furniture store and pick up a few basic items and set it up through the stupid instructions as well as I could, but I still had many leftover pieces that I gave up on.

My place looks nice enough for now. The plan was to stay in, read books, and remain in hiding for a while, but my need for girl's time got the better of me, and I was back in the tunnels and fighting within a week.

I feel awesome.

All the anger hidden underneath my admitted defeat is coming back to the surface with full strength. I am not able to suppress it and don't even want to.

It took about two weeks before I realized that I should have kept it down a notch, as after one of my show-offs in the rink, I was being approached. A guy steps out of the crowd and asks me if I would come over to a casino located on the west side of the city.

He also handed me a stack of money with a picture of a dress that I was to wear, which got me into my defense mode. *Oh, hell, no. You don't tell me what to do dude.*

He spots my look and says, "Pretty please, with a cherry on

the top. Buy it."

I nodded but was turning away from him when I noticed a guy looking straight at me and then turning to speak into his shoulder. I assume there is a phone or radio underneath his coat. *Shit.*

It takes only about five seconds before I spot the lights of approaching cars. I jump over the ropes and start running.

I make it to a parking lot a few blocks away before I see one of the cars turning into the same block that I am on. I slide into one of the open concrete rounds on the ground. *Ouch. Scratched again.*

I feel the burn and then the warmth of blood on the back of my legs. *Damn it.*

I looked from the dark of my hiding spot as the car passed me by within a few seconds.

Here we go. There he is. Four.

Focused on the hunt, he is determined to win, but I won't go easy. I lived in those streets for almost a year before winning the draft and leaving for the base. I know a thing or two around here.

The car stops at the end of the road, about two hundred meters down the hill. Four gets out of the car and opens the back door. Two dogs then jump out of it. *Shit.*

I crawled through the tunnel and start running again. I know where I am heading now, as there is only one way to get rid of the dogs and everybody else.

They reached the end of the bridge just when I pushed myself off into the river. The water swallowed me in. It's fucking freezing, but I keep swimming deep and as far as I can.

When I finally reached the end of my lung capacity, I swam up and got just above the water again enough to see around. I then looked into the far distance. I see people standing on top of the bridge across from me using lights, trying to find me below. Four is one of them.

I would recognize him from anywhere. The way he moves, it's just him and no one else. *Well, cowboy. You are not gonna get me tonight.*

I dive back down into the water and start swimming again to try to get as far away as possible.

Chapter Sixty-Five
Damien – The Message

We get to the lake house basically at the first light as there wasn't anyone able to hold Four back since Rob told him his gun was found in the attic.

Four sprints up the stairs as if being chased, but the gun is just standing there, nicely lined up with the window angle, not going anywhere. When I get there, Four is already kneeling next to it.

"I freaking knew it. Look at the arrogance," he says to me with a smile. "Right under my nose. Boot, you are unbelievable. Oh, wait, look, there is even a message with it."

He then slowly pulled out a piece of paper tucked underneath the scope.

I look at it, but Four needs to translate for me, saying, *"Forgot to watch your back, huh cowboy?"*

He continues to smile happily as an idiot, obviously not getting the point of the message, so I question it with, "Why are we happy about this? The psycho girl wants to put a bullet in your back!"

He is still stupidly excited when answering, "No, dude. If she really wanted that, I wouldn't be breathing anymore. Do you know how many times she's had me in the scope of this gun from here?"

I shook my head and then tried another question. "Okay, does that mean she's gone then? Or where is she now?"

Four rubs his lips together and looks around the room for a bit before something hits, and he adds, "Oh, I see. I better speak to Mia."

With that, he's gone, but I am stopped by the girls in the kitchen.

They are trying to get some info, but I am back to my game of pretending that I am an idiot. *Easy.*

I get on the tractor and pump my way up to the hills with a really good feeling that there isn't any psycho-gunned girl running around the area anymore.

Chapter Sixty-Six

Mia – Coming Clean

"You wouldn't believe it, but guys found my gun at the lake house," Four says to me in the middle of the hockey game he forced me to watch with him.

"Oh, that's good," I say as happily as I can fake it; his face lights up, and he adds right away, "Yes, that is for sure, but it definitely wasn't there about two weeks ago when I was searching through the attic. Your green rain jacket wasn't there either. Interesting right?"

"No, that must have been there, I remember seeing it," I say firmly, but he now turns around to face me fully, which I hate because he reads faces and body language as well as I do with energies.

"No, Mia, it wasn't, and that's really weird, and you know what else is weird? You. Showing up in the kitchen at the lake house while we all know that you can't cook for shit," Four says while moving himself even closer to me to add, "You helped her, I know you did."

"Shh," I say quickly, as Mom keeps moving in the kitchen behind us. His face is literally in mine now when he urges, "What did she say?"

"She was on the run. Some people were after her. Wait, how do you know about the kitchen?"

Four moves away and admits, "Because those people supposedly after her, was me."

I point a finger at him and speak my anger, "I knew it. You hate her."

"Do I?" comes back from him gently, and the only thing I can say at that moment is, "Oh," when I realize how wrong I was reading him before.

That was not hate that I felt. He is falling for the same girl that I am. His energy is very warm and steady now when he speaks about her. He either misses her or worries about her. Maybe both.

I acknowledged, "Well, yes, there was something between you too. Plus, she has the same undertone in words when she speaks as you do. Same country, perhaps? And you might even know each other from there?"

He nods and breathes almost dreamingly, "Yes, I saw her once in the foster care system when we were young, but we met for real only a few weeks ago at the bar."

With that, he moves closer to me again and says, "Mia, Paige is in danger. She knows and has the data that everybody wants. Now, we are going to sit here until you tell me everything you know about where she is now. So, start talking."

Chapter Sixty-Seven

Paige – Zaqua

I learnt my lesson again. How could I be this stupid and keep a fighting routine? Well, that is now over.

The next day, I bought the red dress as requested and went to the casino. I am not entirely happy about this outfit, as I am getting more looks than I thought, but the dress is really beautiful I must say.

The guy who gave me the money was a bodyguard who introduced me to his boss, Ed. We talked, and I agreed that I would accompany him to events as his pretend girlfriend where his bodyguards are not allowed.

We then leave the casino and attend a party on a yacht. The boat is about thirty meters long, a beautiful piece called the Zaqua.

We played pool, Ed played a few rounds of cards, then he dealt with some business, and afterwards he was delivered back to his guards in one piece. *Easy money.*

"You are very beautiful," he adds when I am getting out of his car. I turn back to smile at him and say, "Thank you,". I had a nice evening, which left me in a good mindset, but that feeling changed the exact second my apartment door closed shut behind me.

"So, we meet again Boot," comes from Four, who is now

sitting on my couch in the middle of the room and slowly lifting his eyes up before adding, "Wild look with the white hair, but damn, you look hot as always."

I quickly scan the room but don't see anybody else in here, which means without him knowing how armed I might be, he has the arrogance to fight me alone. *All right then, let's do it.*

I step out of my shoes and walk to the other side of the room. Four's deep voice comes again, saying, "Paige?"

I look at him briefly, and he adds with a heavy tone, "Don't do what you're about to do."

Okay. This stupid dress will limit my kicks, but I am better with my hands anyway. Let's do this.

I start running towards him. After three or four quick steps, I drop down and slide. Four dodges the kick, but I was already on my feet and charging at him with everything I'd got.

"Are you about done?" Four says between covering himself from my hits, but I am too far into it to respond to his arrogance. There. The side of my wrist just got him in the pressure point of his neck, and I feel even more powerful now, but then I realize something is missing. Four is not fighting back.

He hits only defensively, which makes me stop and withdraw, but at that exact moment, he grabs me, pulls me into lips, and now, it's a game over.

The taste I have been craving for weeks raises a wave of emotions that takes over everything. My mind, my senses, and my body. I don't know why he is using me again for his play, but who cares? I need him. I want him.

I feel his body responding under the heat of my hands, which feeds into the energy, knowing that I might not be in control of this, but neither is he.

We are both falling again into the place of complete surrender, approaching each other in a way the other one desires because this is not an encounter of two strangers anymore.

We had intimate moments already. We learned our likes, fantasies, and desires. Four knows where and how to touch me, what makes me surrender to him and I know how to challenge him, bring him to the edge and hold him there for as long as his body can take it.

After about an hour of exhausting ourselves, we are just lying there on the floor of my apartment. Four starts kissing down my stomach then over my belly button ring, which tickles a bit and re-awakens my senses after just shaking uncontrollably from the wave of the last orgasm. He says with a smile in his voice, "I am just thinking. Did you really want to cut me down with my own piece? Pretty savage, I tell you."

"Oh, you mean your gun? Well, you'd deserve it, but even just watching you standing there with your pathetic binoculars while trying to find me was good enough," I say back.

Now Four lifts himself up on one elbow and moves his handsome face above mine before stating, "I knew you were close. I felt your eyes on my back, I swear, but hold on there. What do you mean that I'd deserve it? I've never meant to hurt you. I was trying to help you."

I also lift myself up to argue, "You ordered them to transport me! You were hunting me down! Wait, help me, what do you mean?"

"Yes. To keep you safe. And instead, you've sent two guys to the hospital," Four says and sits up now, but I scoff, "Yeah, to keep me safe. Sure."

Four shakes his head in disbelief. "And what else did you think? I mean, look at me. I am freaking in love with you."

To that, I can't find any words to respond with.

What does he think is going to happen here?

He might have cut a deal with them all, but there is no fairytale ending in this for me. I can't just get discharged and live happily ever after. I know it now, as I knew it when I got in front of the train.

I am done with all of this.

Chapter Sixty-Eight
Mia – The Last Race

I couldn't stop my body shaking the whole day. Finally, we made it to coordinate A and pulled over for the security check. I noticed a few people in the line-up are actually holding guns today. *Crazy.*

Mateo begged me to come, but when he told me they had lost a bookie, he had no idea I knew who he was talking about. *Damn, Paige. I miss you so much.*

Anyway, Chris needs me to help them out, as this is the final race of the season and most important one. However, tonight is definitely different, as two different gangs are attending.

The members of the first one wear masks exposing only eyes and the mouth as usual, which is the gang connected to the RF agency. The members of the Pollwest gang are wearing two bandanas, one that covers the top of their face as hanging from underneath of their hoodie and the second covering the bottom.

The tension between the two gangs is impossible to ignore, even over the music that is louder than the revving engines. I see a lot of people dancing, the crowd is pushing and moving constantly like a flowing river, and the amount of booze and the number of drugs here tonight is beyond reasonable. People around me are doing them without giving a damn if they are being seen, and the energy of it all is pushing me to the point of a breakdown.

We open the wagers, which is great as it gets my brain focusing on something else. The money from the crowds starts flowing in, as well as the online bets. Soon, there are millions in the pot.

I am in the middle of closing a huge transaction when suddenly the loud music disappears completely within the overwhelming noise coming from the crowds.

I see people jumping and stuff being thrown into the air; I hear a broken glass hitting the concrete behind me, people screaming and whistling, and the girls at the front line are freaking out.

"What's happening?" I yelled at Chris, who was counting money beside me. He leans in and yells into my ear, "Four is here."

I lift my eyes up, browse through the crowds, and now I see him.

He has the black and red flag of the Pollwest gang attached to the top of his car while wearing the mask of the RF gang on his head. *Provocative, as always.*

Mateo runs over to us and yells at Chris, "Hey, boss, Four is not looking good. The girls from the bar said he's done so much crystal tonight that he doesn't know who the fuck he is."

Chris nods as if he would expect that and points around with his hand before yelling back at Mateo over the volume of the noise that is not calming down, "But look at the people. They'd freaking die for him."

At this point, Four gets out of his car and brings the crowd's energy to a point of explosion. People are literally throwing themselves at him.

I looked at him again just when two girls started hanging all over him. One of them ripped her top off and was rubbing herself all up against him. While the other girl looks like she was trying to get his pants off. That's when he spotted me and shook them off of him.

Now, he is walking my way, being slowed down by the crowd in his way, but he is getting closer and yelling my way, "Hey Trinity! I am a free man again, let's go fuck."

What the heck?

I am red in the face and so embarrassed with him right now.

"No thanks," I answer quickly, hoping he will turn his attention to someone else. Chris comes to my rescue, gets in front of me, and shouts at Four, "Hey, let her be dude."

Four pushes him away and snaps, "Stay out of it. She fricking loves it on coke. She was begging for it last time."

With that, Four almost reached me. Though, Chris quickly

gets between us to block Four. I admire his courage as Four is out of control; his mind and energy are furious right now, and I don't even recognize him.

At the same time, a guy from the crowd decided to reach out to him for whatever reason, and that was the trigger Four needed to put him over the edge. He throws himself into the crowd, and a fight breaks out. There was no way of stopping it, at least that's what I believed, until Chris walked over to Four's car, pushed the horn down, and held it.

The noise made Four stop after a while, and he is now walking back towards his car.

He spits some blood out but then goes back to smiling. Somewhere along the way, he pauses, turns around, and comes over to me again.

"I'll miss you both," he says and lays a quick kiss on my lips. I didn't even have time to react, but him saying that freaked me out.

With that, he walks over to his car, and the crowd goes wild.

Four stops by his car and is talking to somebody when alias One pulls up, at the speed that he is coming in, he loses control of the steering wheel and scratches Four's car.

Alias One stops and gets out of his car, looking apologetically. Still, Four is already ripping the mask off of his face and storming over to him, "Okay bitch, you wanna go? Let's do it!"

The crowds go wild with the unmasking gesture that can get Four disqualified or even killed. The music disappears again in the uproar, and two other guys jump in front of Four and are now trying to push him towards his car, but he is fighting them all.

Finally, they managed to talk him down, but he still shouted some more words while lifting both arms into the air. I have never been a part of such crowd madness that he created at that moment. The energy overload is unbearable, and I am scared I might pass out.

At the same time, people are throwing money at me, shouting names, and I look at Chris confused because there is no way that I can get any of this in order. I start to type one name of a bet that I understood, but Chris's hand lands on mine. I look at him, and he says, "Don't worry about it, let me handle it."

At that point, the racers were moving over to the start line, and I was only grabbing the money, coming from all sides as there was nothing else that I could do. It was just a mayhem.

Tonight, the bag can barely be zipped up because of the combined amount of money in it from mine and Izzy's side. This is almost triple the amount we normally get.

Then the gun goes and starts the race.

I cover my face from the dust and smoke that is filling the air; Chris takes the money from me, hands me a phone with coordinates of the finish, and gives me the keys to his car.

It's a red convertible that he picked for tonight. I rush over to it, I need to get out of there before the crowds obtain the finish line info, which always makes the traffic unmanageable.

I get on the road, and in about five kilometers, I notice lights in the dark before me. I pull over to see what's going on.

There is a car flipped over onto its roof with a lot of smoke all around it. It looks like the car hit a tree while going off the road, as the front is completely smashed in. The windows are destroyed, but the driver must have flown out of the car as I see nobody inside.

I look around. Over there. A body on the road. Oh my God, Four!

Another three cars are pulling over now; Chris jumps out of the first one and runs over to check on Four.

"I am calling the EMT," I yell after him, and he is screaming back at me, "Fuck, he's not breathing!"

Chris then quickly attempts CPR, but soon Four's car lights on fire and starts burning right behind Chris. People start calling him back to his car, and everyone is leaving the scene in a hurry.

I can't. They are all yelling at me, but I just can't leave.

Four's energy is still with me, and I am not letting it go.

The ambulance must have been nearby, as I then heard the sirens coming down the road towards us.

I see the massive body of the paramedic and some smaller guy getting Four onto the stretcher, and with that, the door closes.

As the ambulance was driving away, Four's car exploded.

Chapter Sixty-Nine

Mia – I Will Miss You Too

"It was a nice service," stated Mom when we got home, but I wasn't listening.

I just couldn't wait to get this black outfit off me. Rob came over and hugged me before whispering into my hair, "It'll sure be different without him."

Then he turns back to our Mom, adding, "But don't let me start on Zeller's. It was a joke. They never really knew Four; they were only trying to find their Thomas in him. Four was his own animal and not just some substitute for their dead son. He deserved better."

Mom nods sadly, but Rob and I are already walking up the stairs to his room. Rob closes the door behind him, and I ask, "Do you actually bring girls in here?" when I see him nodding, I add, "Your hockey bag smells terrible."

"Nah, it's not that bad. You were always so over sensitive to noises, smells, everything."

I wrinkle my nose again. "What kind of girl would have sex with you in here with this god-awful smell?"

He scoffs, "No worries. She doesn't know about any of that when I get it going."

Then he throws his gear into the hockey bag and whispers, "I gotta go. I have to make it to the payphone down at the lake in fifteen minutes."

I react, "And what about me? Does he not wanna talk to me? He better apologize for what he said at the race."

Rob chuckles again, "Oh, come on. You knew Four was gonna say that."

I smile and say, "Yes, but he made it too real."

Then, Rob finished packing up his hockey bag and uttered, "Hey, I really gotta get going now."

I think aloud, "Well, when do you think we'll be able to see them?"

"I dunno, but at least I am getting my invite for sure. Though, I am not a hundred percent about you."

I pull my chin ahead. "What do you mean? I helped. I am the one who had Four as dead in the system before his back even hit the ground."

Rob smiles on the way out, "Yes, but you are also the one who wants to do his girlfriend."

Okay, I can't deny that because it is inevitable. The three of us together. It is going to happen.

"Well, whatever. I am coming with you," I shout and run after him.

Chapter Seventy
Damien – Grandma's

I hope they will come to get me soon, as it wasn't a good idea to come here.

I am sitting on the couch at my Grandma's house, where I haven't been for years. I am under the microscope of four women in their seventies who don't speak a word of English. I understand most of what they say, but I sure am not disclosing that.

This is boring. I want to talk to Rob or Mia. I need to tell them stuff.

The days spent with Four and Rob in the ambulance, learning to act as a paramedic so Mia could call us to the crash scene, was the best fun I've ever had.

I absolutely love and respect Four for who he is, but now, he is giving up his whole life for Paige, and not even Rob could talk him out of it.

I also had my go at Four about that when we were walking into the woods together. He was looking through some bushes for a while before finally finding a black USB stick in a plastic container buried in the ground underneath a pile of rocks.

He turned to me to say, "It is here. I can't believe I am actually holding it."

"What's that?" I had to ask, and Four responded with a face

amazed, "I think she loves me, dude."

"Well, she better," I judged out loud, as, in my eyes, she definitely owes him.

"You don't understand. This is her life. Everyone is looking for this, and she is the key. Thank God she jumped out of that van. I thought I was protecting her, but if she was moved to the base, she would have been killed for this."

"Oh," I acknowledged, and Four added a nod before saying, "She'll be risking more than me at the race. If she gets caught, they get it out of her, and she is dead. And that would be the end of the line for me too. I am not staying a day without her."

I can safely say that he is in love with her.

Four buries the USB stick back into the ground and then adds, "Yo, by the way, we all know you are not an idiot. Mia was reading you this whole time, and she told us you understood what we were saying most of the time, but you didn't come clean, so we decided to fuck with you a bit. Sorry about that."

I smiled and acknowledged, "Wow. Yeah, I forgot about Mia."

"She is like a lie detector, mate, and now, she has the hots for my girl. Same as you do. So, hands off, little buddy, or I will mess you up."

He suddenly didn't look like he was kidding.

"Noted," I said quickly then.

Chapter Seventy-One

Paige – The Night of the Last Race

I can't believe Four talked me into this, but if we want to get out of here together, we need money and a lot of it quickly.

It's super dark outside, and I have been waiting in the forest for about an hour. I am being bitten by millions of mosquitos, getting cold and itchy.

Then, finally, Four sends me the coordinates. I run my eyes through the map and see the curve he picked for the crash. Awesome. It's about five kilometers from my current location.

I start sprinting as fast as my muscles go, but I hope he will make enough of a fuzz at the start line and stall them all for a few extra minutes.

I am about two hundred meters away when I see him flying in, and his car goes rolling. It hits a tree.

Is he okay? There. He is crawling out of the car. There is more blood on him than I expected to see. *Shit.* I feel my chest tightening. *I love him so much.*

Four drops on the ground, but I can't go to him as another car is already coming in. It's Mia.

She gets out of her car, and I move closer as I see other cars also driving up to the scene. Chris stops about fifty meters from me. As predicted, he jumped out of the car and ran over to Four. It was all a matter of seconds, but I was able to quickly open his car door without anyone seeing me. I grabbed the bag of money from all the race bets and ran back to a spot behind some bushes to make sure I was unseen. I quickly looked around, and everything was clear, so I started to run as fast as I possibly could go.

I heard the sirens from the ambulance about a kilometer away when reaching the top of the hill I just conquered. I feel alone and sad, but I can't give in to that. I must keep running.

The train will reach the station in twenty minutes, and I should be there in fifteen at this speed. That will give me five minutes to change clothes and put the money into a waterproof bag to keep it safe.

When I reached the station, I found only an old lady waiting on the platform. She smiled at me, and I smiled back before she said, "Dear, you shouldn't travel alone. People go missing around here."

Then we get on the train. She keeps talking and getting on my nerves, but I am staying in her company anyway as I already see them sitting two rows from us. Don's bodyguards.

They are both looking at me, but the one sitting close to the aisle nods towards the door behind them where he wants me to go. I stay motionless, trying to ignore the gesture while reading their postures. *Can I fight them both? Hardly. Especially the one on the left. He is heavy set but fit.*

They are here for the money, and they are here for me. To drug me again and deliver me back to their boss. The bodyguard on the left is getting impatient. He jerks his thumb towards the door for me to go there, and I nod. There isn't much else I can do. Or is there?

It is too early, but I know my escape route. Plan B.

I got up slowly then but started running towards the other door instead of one they wanted me to go to. I forced it open. The airflow outside is so strong it almost throws me off the train. I grab the ladder on the side of the car and start climbing. The wind on the top is crazy intense, but I run across the roof anyway.

When I got to the middle, I noticed the first of the bodyguards getting on the top at the same point where I came from, but the other one showed up right in front of me on the other side. *Checkmate.*

I am weighing my options.

I must keep them both busy for another few seconds as I already see the lake's reflection in the distance. They are coming close, trying to grab hold of me, and we start fighting. My hands are hitting faster than I ever thought they could as I am going all in.

This is my life. It's now or never.

I kicked the smaller one of them pretty badly and dislocated his kneecap. He is out, gasping in pain, but the other one used the time of my kick to grab my neck, and now he is choking me.

I had only seconds to react. He is strong, and I can't seem to be able to twist myself out of his grip. My lungs are already burning from the lack of oxygen; my sight is slowly leaving me, and suddenly, as if I could hear Four's voice in my head. How many times has he trained me to get out of this? *Come on, you can do it! Think!*

I lift my shoulders up while pulling on the bicep that is squeezing my neck, I am tugging my chin down meanwhile to be able to bite him. I then twist myself out of his hold, step to the side and then go for his vitals. He lets go of me, and I start running.

I then jumped onto the next car and saw the bridge right before us. I look at the water underneath and hear the bodyguard's voice coming from my left. He says mockingly, "You are insane."

I smile at him and take my jacket off, showing the chute attached to my body before saying, "I have been told that before."

Then I start running to the roof's edge and jump.

Chapter Seventy-Two
Mia – What Now?

Rob is driving along the road to the lake, and I am keeping quiet. He doesn't speak either, but he truly doesn't have to. I am reading them all so well now; they are like an open book to me. All of them are, apart from Paige. She is still my big mystery.

She is still the only one who can block me out whenever she wants to. She told me it's not intentional. She has been through a lot, and throughout the years, she must have developed this state of consciousness that works like a shield around her mind. The fact that her and Four were both trained on how to cheat a lie detector adds to it all, I suppose.

And now, what is this? Why are we being pulled over right now?

The police officers approach our car, and we are asked to get out. They run a search through the trunk and back seats. One of them lifts Rob's hockey bag and asks, "Are you playing tonight?"

Rob nods, and the guy points at the black armband on Rob's biceps before saying, "I am sorry about your friend."

"What is this about?" Rob asks back regarding the search, and the guy says, "A cadet failed to return to the base."

Rob asks, "Is he dangerous?"

"She is," answers the guy, but the other officer is looking back at him in a way that he shouldn't have said anything. Then we are free to go.

"Shit. We are late," swears Rob and jumps out of the car the second we stop by the road. He is now sprinting to the ringing phone. I follow, but not as fast as Rob.

When I get there, I lean my ear to the handset of the phone that Rob is holding already. We both wait desperately to hear Four's voice, which then finally comes lazily with, "What's up?

Rob smiles and says, "Ah, not much. Only my best friend died."

Four replies, "Yeah, that sucks, but dude, she's not here."

Rob grabs the phone more to his side now, making me afraid that I won't be able to hear the answer when he asks," What do you mean?"

"They tracked the money. The word on the street is that Paige jumped off the train."

Rob breathes out, "Fuck. You guys really are nuts. Both of you. So, is she okay? Where is she now?"

Four says, "Well, I hope she went for plan B. That means I better get my ass to the airport."

Rob shakes his head and reacts, "Don't. They are

everywhere. Both sides. They have drones in the air and roadblocks at all exits; don't do it. It's a suicide."

Four's voice sends a smile. "Oh, you have not heard. I am dead already."

Chapter Seventy-Three
Damien – Flying Home

Somehow, the flight home seems longer than on the way here.

"Are you not bored by it yet?" I asked Paige while pointing to the movie that has been running on the screen in front of her for a while now, but then I knew the answer before she would even say anything, so I added, "Oh, you were not watching it."

She smiled and looked back at me. The way she moved sent a whiff of her perfume all the way to my nostrils, and that didn't help with the fact how attracted to her I already was.

Shit. I should say something clever. She doesn't look nervous, but she must be. If she doesn't pass the passport stamp, they will transport her back and probably kill her.

"I miss him too," was the only thing that came out of my mouth. I am such an idiot.

I have not been close to people like her or Four before. I have read about them and seen movies, but that is all different now as she is just a girl.

Just a girl sitting next to me on the plane, who could probably seriously harm most of us before being detained, but to the guy across the aisle from me who had been giving me a thumbs up since the take-off, she is just a dream.

"Four is everything," Paige says, and I must add, "That's

exactly what he said about you."

Damn, I am staring at her again.

Even the way she sits is unusual. Her body is not as stiff as mine after being squeezed into an uncomfortable plane seat. Her body is awake. Always. And it makes me sad as that is one of the things right in my face showing how out of my league she actually is.

I couldn't believe my eyes when I saw her parachuting from the top of the bridge in the middle of the night. That was some James Bond type of shit.

I was waiting there, smoking a joint and chilling by myself, not thinking that we would ever need to go with plan B, but then the train came, and I saw her jumping. My heart was beating like crazy the whole time. Then she got out of the water and followed me to Four's car. She drove me back to Grandma's, and I then packed my luggage with the money that Paige had given me. I wanted her to sleep over, but she had to take care of some stuff in the city, and I didn't see her again until I got on the plane. Damn, how beautiful she is.

Now, my ears are plugging and unplugging, so I know we are landing soon. I don't like the moments before the plane hits the ground, but all went well.

We are now standing together in the line-up for the passport stamps. Paige leans to me and says, "If this goes wrong, please give him this, will ya?"

I see the message on the paper she placed into my hand; no

one needs to translate for me anymore. It says, "I'll see you on the other side, cowboy."

Then we move. Paige approaches the booth with the guy on the left side, and I get the lady on the right. I smile at Paige, and the lady officer asks me, "Are you traveling together?"

"Yes. She is my stepsister," I lied but noticed Paige's passport being stamped at the same time.

Interesting. Her passport has the same color as mine. Oh, there you have it. She was flying home, I guess.

Once I walked through the booths, she was already waiting for me on the other side.

She has sunglasses on now and a baseball cap with a hoodie over it.

She then starts pulling me into moving, so we start walking. She leans in and whispers, "There are cameras everywhere. Just put your arm around me, okay?"

Sure. Four will probably kill me for touching her, but every second of it was worth it.

Then we got outside the airport, and I realized she put her passport into my other hand. Unfortunately, she also gestured for me to take my arm off from around her. Damn. I wish I could keep touching her.

I am just turning to her to say something clever, but there I see her eyes running over the other side of the street where people are peacefully jumping into the cabs. With that, Paige lets go of my hand.

I looked around, confused, and then I looked back at her, but she wasn't there anymore. As if the crowd swallowed her. I look back hysterically to where she looked before and now see two men running along the road, who would, with their looks in suits, pass for some agents or bodyguards.

My eyes start twitching between the crowds, searching through them desperately, but it seems as if none of this has ever happened.

Paige is gone.

About The Author

Cara Biceffi is an enthusiastic and athletic person who always finds something to do. After the birth of her first son, she was very eager to try something new and decided to write a story that she was holding back on.

Usually, Cara likes to go mountain biking, driving and she is enjoying any other activity that makes her feel energized.

With some persuasion from her friends, she decided to put together all the activities she likes into a fictional story for you all to read.